THE 1864 CIVIL WAR DIARY AND BRIEF BIOGRAPHY OF JAMES B. ESSIG

Thomas A. Marquard

Printed by Lulu Press, Inc. www.lulu.com
Printed in U.S.A

ISBN: 978-1-4357-5775-2

Library of Congress Control Number: 2008908995

CONTENTS

For All of His Great Grandchildren and Their Children and Grandchildren to Come.......

LIST OF ILLUSTRATIONS/PHOTOGRAPHS

Introduction & Background

My great grandfather James B. Essig was the grandfather of my mother, Elizabeth Gertrude Marquard nee Wertz. He was the father of my grandmother, Laura Gaily Wertz, nee Essig, affectionately known to us grandchildren as “Amba”. James’ death certificate shows his father as William, who was born in Pennsylvania, and his mother as Rebecca Rimus, birthplace unknown. The Department of the Interior Bureau of Pensions contains a document **(see figure 1)** signed by Essig wherein he states his date of birth as September 26, 1841, born at Greentown in Stark Co., Ohio.

Family lore (primarily from my mother) held that he joined the Ohio Volunteers as a drummer boy at the age of 16. However, National Archive records **(see figure 2**) show him as enlisting in 104th Ohio Volunteer Infantry **(see figure 3)** Company F, I, at the age of 20 on August 2, 1862. He was mustered in August 30, 1862 at Camp Massillon, Ohio. Records show him as 5 foot 10 inches with brown hair and blue eyes. His home is listed as Randolph in Portage County, Ohio and his occupation, farmer. **(See figures 4, 5 & 6).**

While Essig enlisted as a Private the records show him being promoted to Corporal by order of Colonel Reilly in June of 1863. There is an additional record that shows him as belonging to the 19th Regiment Veteran Reserve Corp with a rank of Corporal. This regiment was formed January 12, 1864 in Washington D.C. and was mustered out after the war’s end by detachments from 7/13-11/16/1865. He would have transferred to this regiment due to disability from his wound in 1863.

3—389

DEPARTMENT OF THE INTERIOR
BUREAU OF PENSIONS

WASHINGTON, D. C., *January 2, 1915.*

SIR: Please answer, at your earliest convenience, the questions enumerated below. The information is requested for future use, and it may be of great value to your widow or children. Use the inclosed envelope, which requires no stamp.

Very respectfully,

G M Saltzgaber
Commissioner.

JAMES ESSIG
CARROLLTON OHIO
123308

PENSION
L
MAR
22
1915
U. S.
OFFICE.

No. 1. Date and place of birth? *Answer.* Greentown Stark Co O. Sep 26 1841

The name of organizations in which you served? *Answer.* Co. I 104 Regt O.V.I.

No. 2. What was your post office at enlistment? *Answer.* Randolph Portage Co Ohio

No. 3. State your wife's full name and her maiden name. *Answer.* Elizabeth McCormick Essig Elizabeth McCormick

No. 4. When, where, and by whom were you married? *Answer.* Aug. 12 1869 Hanoverton Columbiana Co Ohio Rev. John W Wright M.E. Preacher

No. 5. Is there any official or church record of your marriage? by pastor John W. Wright

If so, where? *Answer.* Have in our possession Marriage License signed

No. 6. Were you previously married? If so, state the name of your former wife, the date of the marriage, and the date and place of her death or divorce. If there was more than one previous marriage, let your answer include all former wives. *Answer.* not previously married

No. 7. If your present wife was married before her marriage to you, state the name of her former husband, the date of such marriage, and the date and place of his death or divorce, and state whether he ever rendered any military or naval service, and, if so, give name of the organization in which he served. If she was married more than once before her marriage to you, let your answer include all former husbands. *Answer.* not married before her marriage to me

No. 8. Are you now living with your wife, or has there been a separation? *Answer.* living with my first wife no separation

No. 9. State the names and dates of birth of all your children, living or dead. *Answer.*

Emma Lee Essig Born May 20 1870
Mary Anderson Essig Born March 5 1872
Anna Grace " " Aug 28 1875
Lillian Alice " " Aug 3 1882
Laura Gailey " " Nov 2 1886

Date .... *(Signature)* James Essig

Figure 1 Dept of Interior Doc. 1915 (ref. page 1 & 105)

104 | Ohio.

...es Essig

...I, 104 Reg't Ohio Infantry.

... Muster-out Roll, dated

... H C, June 17, 1865.

... June 17, 1865.

... Oct. 31, 1863.

...31, 1864; drawn since $......100

......100; due U. S. $......100

... kind or money adv'd $......100

...ns, equipments, &c., $......100

...5 100; due $ 75 100

... paid $96 ... for ... of Sept. Oct. Nov. ...64 and Jany. Feb. 1865

...80 1869

(over)

... Copyist.

E | 104 19 | Ohio V. R. C.

James X Essing

Corp., Co. H, 19 Reg't Veteran Res. Corps.

Appears on

Company Muster Roll

for May & June 1864

Present or absent

Stoppage, $......100 for

Due Gov't, $......100 for

Co. and Reg't from which transferred

Remarks: Trans'f'd June 19/64 by order Sec. of War 207. to Co. I. 104 O. V. I.

Book mark:

Sewell Copyist.

(358)

E | 104 | Ohio.

James Esigg

Co. I, 104 Reg't Ohio Infantry.

Appears on

Company Descriptive Book

of the organization named above.

DESCRIPTION.

Age 20 years; height 5 feet 10 inches.

Complexion Light

Eyes Blue; hair Brown

Where born Randolph Portage Co O.

Occupation Farmer

ENLISTMENT.

When Aug 2, 1862.

Where Randolph Portage Co O

By whom Capt Wells; term 3 y'rs.

Remarks: Taken prisoner at Danville Ky Mch 24 63 & escaped same day. Promoted to Corpl by Order Col. Reilly June 1863 Wounded through face Nov 29, 63 at Siege of Knoxville (Over)

(888) Holtzman Copyist.

Figure 2 Company Book doc. 1869 (ref. page 1)

104th Regiment, Ohio Infantry

UNION OHIO VOLUNTEERS

104th Regiment, Ohio Infantry

Organized at Camp Massillon, Ohio, and mustered in August 30, 1862. Moved to Covington, Ky., September 1, 1862. Attached to 2nd Brigade, 1st Division, Army of Kentucky, Dept. of the Ohio, to November, 1862. 2nd Brigade, 2nd Division, Army of Kentucky, to January, 1863. 1st Brigade, District of Central Kentucky, Dept. of Ohio, to June, 1863. 2nd Brigade, 1st Division, 23rd Army Corps, Dept. of Ohio, to July, 1863. 2nd Brigade, 4th Division, 23rd Army Corps, to August, 1863. 1st Brigade, 3rd Division, 23rd Army Corps, Army Ohio, to February, 1865, and Dept. of North Carolina, to June, 1865.

SERVICE.-Defence of Cincinnati, Ohio, against Kirby Smith's threatened attack September 2-12, 1862. Skirmish at Fort Mitchell, Covington, Ky., September 10. Pursuit to **Lexington**, Ky., September 12-15. Duty at Lexington till December 6. Moved to Richmond and Danville, Ky., in pursuit of Morgan December 6-26. At Frankfort, Ky., till February, 1863. Operations in Central Kentucky till August. Expedition to Monticello and operations in Southeastern Kentucky April 26-May 12. Burnside's Campaign in East Tennessee, Campaign August 16-October 17. Expedition to Cumberland Gap September 4-7. Operations about Cumberland Gap September 7-10. Knoxville Campaign November 4-December 23. Siege of Knoxville November 17-December 5. Duty in East Tennessee till April, 1864. **Atlanta** (Ga.) Campaign May 1 to September 8. Demonstration on **Rocky Faced Ridge** and Dalton, Ga., May 8-13. Battle of **Resaca** May 14-15. Cartersville May 20. Operations on line of Pumpkin Vine Creek and battles about **Dallas**, **New Hope Church** and Allatoona Hills May 25-June 5. Operations about Marietta and against Kenesaw Mountain June 10-July 2. Skirmishes about Lost Mountain June 11-14. Combats about Lost Mountain June 15-17. Muddy Creek June 17. Noyes Creek June 19. Cheyney's Farm June 22. Ulley's Farm June 26-27. Assault on **Kenesaw** June 27. Nickajack Creek July 2-5. Chattahoochie River July 5-17. Buckhead, Nancy's Creek, July 18. **Peach Tree Creek** July 19-20. Siege of **Atlanta** July 22-August 25. **Utoy Creek** August 5-7. Flank movement on Jonesboro August 25-30. Battle of **Jonesboro** August 31-September 1. Lovejoy Station September 2-6. Operations against Hood in North Georgia and North Alabama September 29-November 3. **Nashville** Campaign November-December. **Columbia**, Duck River, November 24-27. Columbia Ford November 28-29. Battle of **Franklin** November 30. Battle of Franklin December 15-16. Pursuit of Hood to the Tennessee River December 17-28. At Clifton, Tenn., till January 15, 1865. Movement to Washington, D, C., thence to Federal Point, N. C., January 15-February 9. Operations against Hoke near Fort Fisher February 11-14. Orton's Pond February 18. **Fort Anderson** February 18-19. **Town Creek** February 19-20. Capture of **Wilmington** February 22. Campaign of the Carolinas March 1-April 26. Advance on Goldsboro March 6-21. Occupation of Goldsboro March 21. Advance on Raleigh April 10-14. Occupation of Raleigh April 14. Bennett's House April 26. Surrender of Johnston and his army. Duty at Raleigh till May 2, and at Greensboro till June. Mustered out June 17, 1865.

Regiment lost during service 3 Officers and 46 Enlisted men killed and mortally wounded and 4 Officers and 130 Enlisted men by disease. Total 183.

http://www.itd.nps.gov/cwss/template.cfm?unitname=104th%20Regiment%2C%20Ohio%... 2/21/2006

Figure 3 104th Ohio Record (ref. page 1)

Figure 4 Unrestored Tintype of Essig (ref. page 1)

Figure 5 Restored Tintype (ref. page 1)

Figure 6 Undated Early Photo (ref. page 1)

1863 Capture and Wounding

My mother said that Essig was captured by the Rebels and imprisoned but subsequently escaped from Andersonville Prison in Georgia, with the help of a "Negro Mammy". This appears very unlikely as this infamous prison operated from February 1864 to early 1865. We know from the diary where he was in 1864 however, it is possible he could have somehow ended up there in early 1865. I have researched the Andersonville prisoner roster and his name is not listed.

Although there's no mention of Andersonville, the National Archive records do reveal that James was "taken prisoner at Danville, KY March 24, 63 & escaped the same day." Based on the records it appears he was near Danville, KY at this time fighting Rebel raiders, probably Mosby's brigade. This is the only reference to him being captured that I was able to find.

Family accounts also said that he was shot in the cheek and that the Minie ball **(see figure 7)** remained imbedded there until the day he died on May 3, 1918. The National Archive records confirm that "he was wounded through the face Nov. 29, 1863 at the Siege of Knoxville, Tenn." His military pension records contain a sworn affidavit from 1872 which describes the circumstances of his wound as follows:

> "The wound was received about November 29, 1863. Applicant was with his company and regiment on the south side of river, four companies of his regiment were in advanced line defending our line against charge of the enemy when he received a ball in the left cheek about three fourths of an inch below the left eye which passed through the face under eyes and lodged in the right side of

the face over the lower jaw and now remains embedded in the right side of the head."

This battle took place in Knoxville, TN on November 29, 1863 at what is alternately referred to as "The Battle or Siege of Knoxville" or "The Assault on Ft. Sanders". Ft. Sanders is also known as Ft. Loudon **(see figures 8 & 9)**. It was an important Union victory.

His wound was quite serious and the records reflect his almost continuous treatment at hospitals in Knoxville and later at Camp Dennison in Ohio **(see figure 16)**. His military pension records contain an "Examining Surgeon's Certificate" dated November 19, 1875 and signed by William Tripp, Examining Surgeon, which states:

> "Gunshot wound of the left molar bone – ball entered immediately beneath the external cauthus of the orbit of the left eye - passing diagonally through the molar bone and internal nasal cavity and lodged beneath the right eye where it still remains."

The wound caused him great pain and partial disability for the rest of his life. He comments periodically throughout the diary on the discomfort, but never really complains much considering the gravity of the wound and the general hardships of military life. I will comment on the affects of the wound on his life after the war toward the end of this book.

1864 Prologue

James Essig was furloughed to home on February 2, 1864 returning to veteran invalid duty on March 1st when the diary really begins. Throughout 1864 he was assigned at or near various military hospitals mainly in Ohio, Washington D.C. and in Tennessee. Although he was considered an "invalid" he still performed military service including guard duty, hospital work and cook. He marched and drilled frequently. He was often called to arms and was ready to fight; although it is not clear to what extent he participated in the actual hostilities of 1864. Nonetheless, I found the diary to be a very interesting first-hand account of a Civil War soldier and an eyewitness to history, including the 1864 election of Lincoln and Johnson. Johnson happened to be the military Governor of Tennessee in Nashville where Essig spent much of 1864.

Essig was also an "accidental tourist", spending the first part of the year in and around Washington D.C., mostly on guard duty as part of the city's defenses. He saw many sights including the building of the Washington Monument, and made many visits to the "new" Smithsonian Museum **(see figure 10)**. While there he spent much of his free time in the Senate and House listening to speeches and saw many of the politicians and celebrities of the time.

The records also place him at or very near to the battles of Franklin and Nashville in Tennessee, which took place in late 1864. He comments on the Battle of Franklin, one of the bloodiest of the war. The diary also confirms his presence in Nashville while that battle raged. It is noteworthy that all of the major battles (Knoxville, Franklin & Nashville) that we know he was involved in were great and strategic victories for the Union. The Battles of Franklin (11/30/1864 see diary entry) and Nashville (see entries 12/1-22) hastened the end of the war and forced Lee's surrender in April of 1865 **(see figures 11 & 12)**.

I was also told by my Mother that Essig was with General William Tecumseh Sherman on his famous or some would say infamous "March to the Sea". There is evidence that he may have served under Sherman in Kentucky. Sherman was also the General in charge of the campaign of which he served in Nashville. It is entirely likely he rejoined his old regiment with Sherman late in 1864 or early 1865. He would have missed Atlanta (Sept.1864) but could have linked up in Savannah and fought in the Carolina campaigns. The records show that he was not mustered out until late 1865 so it is plausible that he was with Sherman. The diary ends abruptly on December 23, 1864 when he was on his way home for furlough and missed his train connection near Louisville.

Figure 7 Minie Balls .54-69 Cal. (ref. page 8)

Figure 8 Rebel Charge on Ft. Sanders (above) and Battle of Knoxville (ref. page 9)

Figure 9 Assault on Ft. Sanders (ref. page 9)

Figure 10 The Smithsonian in 1860s (ref. page 10)

Figure 11 The Battle of Franklin (ref. page 11)

Figure 12 The Battle of Nashville (ref. page 11)

Diary Description

The diary was given to me by my Mother in the early 1960s because of my long time interest in Great Grandfather Essig and the American Civil War. It was in very good condition when first viewed by me, but due to age and handling, is now faded and in tatters. I thought it best to transcribe it, to the extent possible, before it is lost to posterity. It is 3" X 5" and was clad in thin leather (only the back cover remains) with a leather tongue and loop clasp. I've included some photographs **(see figures 13, 14 & 15)** to supplement this document. It is written in various inks and pencil. Much has faded and is illegible or required some guesswork. I have added in parentheses question marks or other notes in the text where I was unable to decipher his writings or to aid in understanding his meaning. In some cases, for clarity's sake, I have corrected the original spelling, syntax or punctuation.

Great Grandfather Essig's writings portray a deeply religious, patriotic, and well-read young man who often is suffering from not only his wound but the general trials and tribulations of a soldier of his time. It is evident that he longed for the war to end so he might return safely to his home, family and friends.

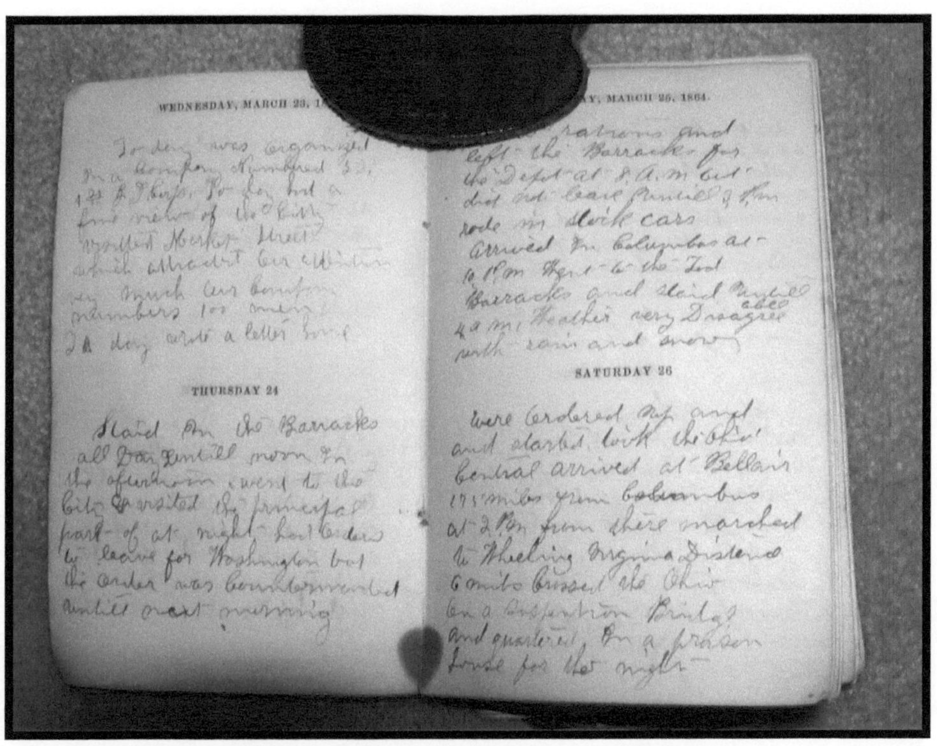

Figure 13 Photo of diary (ref. page 18)

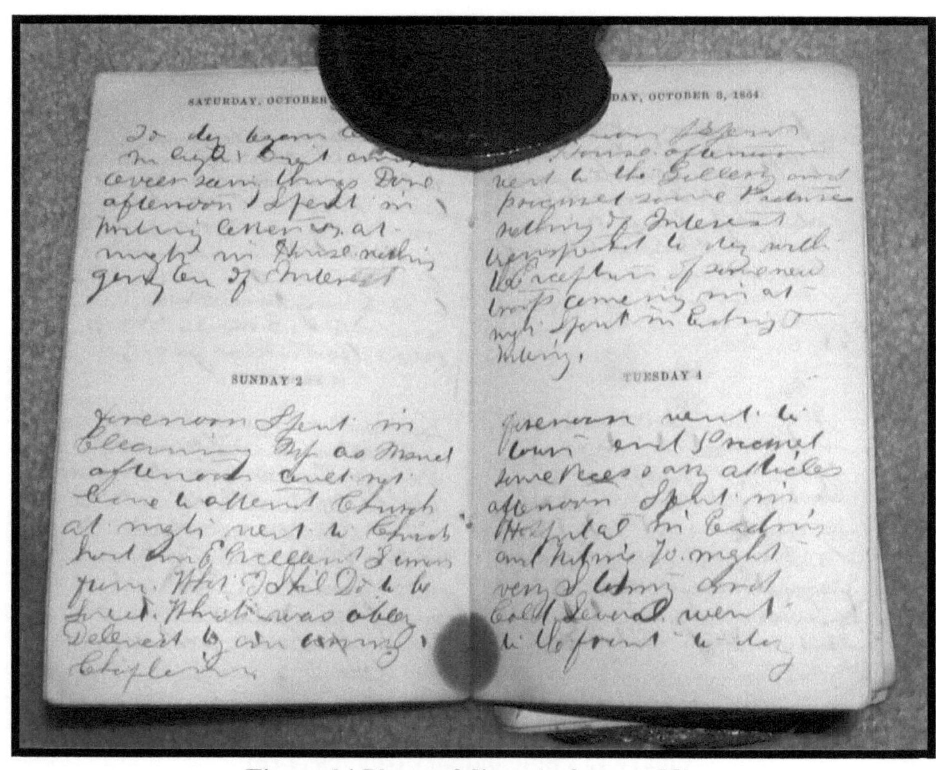

Figure 14 Photo of diary (ref. page 18)

Figure 15 Doodles in diary (ref. page 18 & 94)

Diary Text

On the first page under the date Jan. 1, he wrote:

"This is the property of James Essig, bought Feb. the 22nd, 1864 in Ravenna, price 65 cts" and then signed *"James Essig"*.

My research has discovered a statement written by his wife, after his death, that he actually was not given a middle name or initial. She wrote that he felt he needed one after entering college, in the late 1860s, so he chose the initial "B". I don't know if it stood for anything.

The next several pages contained a monthly almanac for 1864 showing the moon's phases and tides by day of the week. The following pages contain Cash Accounts and Memorandum.

In the memorandum pages he has listed accounts of people that owe him money totaling under $50. He also lists his expenses:

Great Coat	*$19.50*
Blouse	*3.12*
Pants	*6.00*
Shirts	*2.50*
Socks, blankets, tents, dress coat - no prices	
Drawers	*1.50*
Canteen	*1.31*
Jacket, Invalid	*4.25*
Blouse	*2.45*
Etc. Total	*$30.71*

In the pages prior to Feb 22 he notes distances traveled:

Distances Traveled
1862 - 325 miles

> *"Distance traveled in the year 1863 from Knoxville Tennessee to Jonesborough 260 miles"*
> *"Distance from Knoxville to home 1100, from home to Camp Dennison 800 miles to Cincinnati 16 miles. From Cincinnati to Washington 700 miles, Washington to Cincinnati 700 miles...* (Illegible)"

Table of Distances

Distances from different cities in Kentucky and Tennessee.

From Covington to Lexington 100
Lexington to Richmond 126
Richmond to Danville 34
Danville to Frankfort 50
Danville to Lexington 28
Lexington to Craborchard 5
Craborchard to Mt. Vernon 12
Lexington to (?) *60*
Danville to Knoxville 300
Knoxville to Cumberland Gap 64
Knoxville to Jonesborough 125
Knoxville to Chattanooga 200
Chattanooga to Nashville 350 (?)
Nashville to Louisville 194
Jeffersonville to Seymore 60
Seymore to Cincinnati 120
Cincinnati to Columbus 120

Columbus to Zanesville 48
Cressline to Columbus 60
Cressline to Alliance 105
Zanesville to Wheeling 120
Wheeling to Harpers Ferry 120
Harpers Ferry to Washington Junction 60
Washington to Baltimore 41
Washington to Harrisburg, PA 120
Washington to Alexandria 6
Chattanooga to Atlanta 150

The next page contains a *"List of Books Read in the yr.62 at Camp Denison"*

3 Yrs. On (on or in?) *Chlr* (?)
Revelation of Rights
Life and Travels in Brazil (?)
Washington the Young Men's Guide
4 Yrs. In Great Britain
History of England
Nashville, Tenn.
Baxter's Call to the Wren (?)
Edward Payson
Oct 12th on Clerical Manners

Quotations

"The time for reasoning is before you approach near enough to the forbidden fruit to look and admire"
"Study your character and future prospects"

Curiosities witnessed in the City of Washington

At the patent office saw Washington's personal effects and also presentations from all parts of the world. In the center of the building stands a monument now partly completed. We also saw some of the clothing worn by Dr. Franklin in the Artic (?) *Expedition and also a primitive press used by him in England. And also saw patents of all descriptions ever known to be on exhibition. The building covers the space of 2 squares.*

Incidents Concerning the Capitol

The first thing that attracts our attention as we enter is the illustrations (life-size) *of the discovery of America by Columbus in 1492. Surrender of Cornwallis & Burgoyne to General Washington. Life size of General Scot on horse-back. Discovery of Mississippi by Desoto and the erection of a monument in the year 1541.*

The Capitol is comprised of the Executive and Senate and House of Representatives. Each about 100 by 80 feet in dimensions. Left Washington (?).

The Capitol is located on P.A. Ave. and Capitol Hill. Treasury building on 14th St. north. Post Office on 4K St. Smithsonian Institute on 7th St. South.

Items of Interest and Historical Interest

London contains at present 459 chapels of different denominations.

2nd. the number of criminals committed to prison in London between the yrs. 1821 & 27 was 19,833.

3rd. historically there are 19 tunnels between Wheeling & Washington some over a mile long.

Facts from History

1st Queen of Babylon: Semiramus. Founder of Babylonian Empire: Nimrod.

Commencement of line. History 770 yrs.B.C. 1st King of Persia: Cyrus 747. The Army of Herod preparing for the crushing of Grecian Empire founded 1000 yrs.B.C.

Four largest cities of Greece follow: Athens, Sparta, Sebes and Argus. Socrates born at Athens, Greece. 470 B.C. Alexander's first invasion of Persia.

Chronology of England

Caesar's first invasion of Britain: 55 B.C. Second invasion 54 B.C. Claudius takes an expedition to Britain 43 B.C. First arrival of Saxons in England A.D. 450.Yellow Plague 664. England unites all the...A. D 827.Anglo Saxon Kingdom's Descent of James 827 A.D. Accession of Albert 871. Alfred's treaty with James 878. Death of Alfred 901. Massacre of James 1002. Accession of Canute 1017. Death of Edward Confessor 1066. Accession of William Rufus 1087. Henry conquers Normandy and carries his brother Robert to England. Death of Henry - Stephen seizes the vacant throne 1135.Stephen defeated and captured - Matilda takes throne 1141. Death of Stephen accession of Henry II 1154. Conquest of Ireland 1171.Death of Henry - accession of Richard I - 1189. Persecution and massacre of Pens. Richard seized and confined in Germany 1192. Death of Richard 1199. Accession of King John 1199. Magna Charter granted 1272. Parliament of Oxford 1258.

Accession of Edward I 1272, Conquest of Wales 1283, Jews banished from England 1290 Conquest of Scotland, Wallace executed in London 1305. Accession of Edward II 1307, Queen Isabella invades England and displaces her husband 1326, King murdered in Berkley Castle 1327, Accession of Edward III 1327, Naval Victory over French at Sluys 1340, Carlos taken 1347, and Great pestilence 1349.

The French King defeated and confined by the Black Prince 1356. Another pestilence 1361. Death of Black Prince 1376. Death of Edward III accession of Richard II 1377.

Henry IV crowned 1399. Death of Henry IV accession of Henry V 1413. Treaty of Isiz 1420. Death of Henry V accession of Henry VI 1422. Siege of Orleans - Joan of Arc 1429. The English expelled from France 1451. Insurrection of Duke of York 1452. Commencement of Civil Wars 1455. Battle of Wakefield. Date of death of Duke of York 1460. Edward IV declared King of Citizens of London 1461. Edward IV assumes the crown - Battle of Lawton 1461.

Henry IV imprisoned in the Tower 1466. Warwick invades England and releases Henry IV 1470 and Edward returns and defeats Warwick 1471. Duke of Clarence put to death 1478. Death of Edward IV accession of Edward V 1483. The Earl of Richlands (?) defeats and (?) Richard at Bosworth and assumes the Crown1485. Henry VII marries Elizabeth of York1486. Lambert Simnel impersonates Edward Earl of Nanykond (?) pretends crown (?) 1487. Death of Henry VII accession of Henry VIII.

Battle of Flodden Field 1513, Wolsey Cardinal and chanse (?) 1515, Death of Cardinal Wolsey 1530. Henry VIII marries Elizabeth of York and unites Chims (?) of Lancaster 1486. Henry marries Anne Boleyn 1533. Execution of Bishop (?). Thomas More Wales incorporates English laws 1535. Anne Boleyn executed 1536. Birth of Edward VI 1537. Capture of Bolings (?) 1544. Execution of the King 1547.

Edward VI proclamation for removal of images 1548. Liturgy reformed 1549. Summerset beheaded 1552. Death of Edward VI 1553. Coronation of Queen Elizabeth, restoration of the (?) church 1559. Queen Mary returns to Scotland 1561. Mary of Scots in to England is brought to trial and detained a prisoner 1568. Duke of Norfolk executed for treason 1572.

Queen of Scots executed Feb. 8, 1587. Expedition to Cadiz 1596.Conspiracy and execution of Essex 1601. Death of Elizabeth 1603. Accession of James I, conspiracy to place Isabella Stuart on the throne 1603. Hampton Court 1604, Gunpowder Plot 1605, Jamestown, Virginia founded 1607. Accession of Charles 1st 1625. The Covenant established in Scotland 1638.

Scots invaded England 1640. Impeachment of Strafford 1640. Act and execution of Strafford 1641. Accusation of Lord Wimbledon and the five members of his ring set his standard at Nottingham 1622. Trial & execution of King Charles 1649. Charles II and Parliament at Edinburgh 1649. England declares a Commonwealth 1649. Charles II lands at Scotland 1650. Charles II crowned at Scotland. Invades England escapes to France 1651. War with Holland 1652.

1653, Cromwell's first Parliament. Parliament expelled. Cromwellian Protection. 1653 Defeat of Dutch Death of Cromwell second Parliament. Cromwell refuses (?) 1656. Dunkirk taken & Cromwell's death. His son Richard declared Lord Protector. General Monk (?) enters England from Scotland. Restoration of Church 1660. Act of Uniformity passed 1662. Covenanters Act 1665. Plague in London 1665.

Great sea fights 1666, against the Dutch fleet. (?) *Insults Chatham. Fall of Clarendon 1667. Death of Charles II 1685. Reign 25 yrs. Accession of James II 1685. Attack on privileges of the* (?) *1687. Trial of Bishop* (?) *by Prince* (?) *of Holland. King William & Mary proclaimed 1689. Battle of Boyne 1690. Massacre of Glencoe 1692. Commencement of the Spanish succession 1701. Death of William 1712. Accession and coronation of Queen Anne 1702. Gibraltar taken 1704. Union with Scotland 1708.*

Death of Queen Anne 1714. Accession of George 1714. Death of Louis IV 1715. Accession of Geo. II 1727. War declared against Spain 1739. War declared by France against England 1744. Reformation of calendar 1652. Pitt's first administration commencement of 7 yrs. War 1757. Cherbourg destroyed 1758. Canada conquest death of George II 1760. The family contract between George and Naples 1761. Peace of Paris end of 7 yrs. War 1762. Grenville's American Stamp Act 1765. Repeal of the American Stamp Act 1766. An act to levy tax on tea and other articles in America 1767.

Resignation of (?) *1768. Repeal of the taxes imposed on American exports-tea 1769. Popular outbreak at Boston 1773. Commencement of the American Revolution 1775. Capitulation of Saratoga 1777. Alliance with America with France 1778. Peace of Versailles 1783. Impeachment of Hastings 1786. Outbreak of French Revolution 1789. French expedition to Egypt 1798. Nelson's victory over French Navy 1798. Failure of British expedition to Holland 1799. Irish Rebellion 1799.* (?) *with Ireland 1800. Peace of Armens* (?) *Battle of Copenhagen 1801. 1802. Bonaparte Consul for life 1802.*

Diary by Date

The following is my transcription of James Essig's diary which doesn't actually start until March 1st. The first dated entry is wedged in his "Chronology of England between 1656 and 1660". It reads:

Feb 2nd

Today we come from Ravenna and this afternoon staid (sic) *at home.*

Tuesday March 1, 1864

Left home enroute for the regiment. Started from Rootstown Station at 3PM. Arrived at Alliance at 3:30. Started at 6PM and arrived at Columbus at 4AM Wednesday.

Wednesday 2

Procured an order from the Provost Marshal and reported to Fort Stanton for examination and was then sent to this Seminary Hospital. Remained there 2 hours and then was ordered to Camp Dennison. Started about 2 PM arrived in camp at 8PM

Thursday, March 3, 1864

Today spent in Camp Dennison **(see figure 16)**. *For the first time wrote two letters home and went to visit Duane Austin.*

Friday 4

Nothing of any importance transpired. Spent all of my time in reading and writing, weather very pleasant, prospects for rain.

Saturday, March 5, 1864

Weather very sultry, some rain. Spent my time in reading a book entitled "The Revelation of Rights".

Sunday 6

Spent the first part of day in Camp Dennison. Went to meeting (note: generally his use of "meeting" refers to a church service) *at 10 ½* (10:30) *and 2PM. Heard an excellent discourse delivered by Chaplain of the 53rd 6rg.*

Monday, March 7, 1864

Forenoon spent in reading, afternoon went to visit the 12, 6 v, C. Weather very pleasant at night went to Church.

Tuesday 8

Forenoon spent in camp reading and amusing ourselves as well as we could. Afternoon went to the depot in company with D.S. Austin, had a good time. In the evening went to Church.

Wednesday, March 9, 1864

Forenoon spent in reading, afternoon went the depot and saw trains coming in loaded with soldiers, principally veterans.

Thursday 10

Weather very disagreeable rained all day. Spent the time in house. At night went to Church and heard Chaplain Griffith of the 50th OVP preach.

Friday, March 11, 1864

Weather more pleasant and only some colder today. Made some rings and at night went to Church. Today 3 regiments went to the front through this place.

Saturday 12

Spent part of the time in reading and went to the depot and saw the Battery T.1st 6 V Artillery return to the front - as veterans and recruits.

Sunday, March 13, 1864

Weather quite cold, went to Church at 10AM and 2PM. At night listened to a sermon in the evening from Chaplain Sullivan from the 70th 6VP.

Monday 14

Weather cold and snow this morning. Was examined by the Invalid board and put in the 1st Battalion Invalid Corp.

Tuesday, March 15, 1864

Weather very stormy, went to the Depot and saw the 70th OVP go to the front. In the evening went to church.

Wednesday 16

Today was spent mostly in the house as it was very cold. 3 regiments departed for the front, the 33

& 31st 6vp. At night went to church and heard a soldier preach by the name of Stewart.

Thursday, March 17, 1864

Weather very cold, wrote one letter and at night went to meeting. Last night a soldier was thrown from the cars (note: refers to railroad cars) and instantly killed.

Friday 18

Weather quite cold, nothing of any importance transpired only the departure of troops to the front.

Saturday March 19, 1864

Forenoon done some washing, in the afternoon went to visiting. At night spent the time in reading; "The Life of Dr. Livingstone: 3 Yrs. In Africa", and also wrote a letter home.

Sunday 20

Weather very cold, went to church at 10 AM and heard the Chaplain preach. At night heard a strange preacher, a local preacher connected with the Army.

Monday, March 21, 1864

Weather very cold stayed in the house most of the day. At night went to church and heard Mr. Firz preach.

Tuesday 22

Suffered in the morning with a pain in my head. At noon received orders to go to Cincinnati. When *we arrived at night, went to the barracks and spent a very cold night of it.*

Wednesday, March 23, 1864

Today was organized in a Company numbered 53, 1st J, I Corps. Today had a fine view of the city, visited Market Street which attracted our attention very much. Our Company numbers 100 men. Today wrote a letter home.

Thursday 24

Stayed in the barracks all day until Noon. In the afternoon went to the city and visited the principal part of it at night. Had orders to leave for Washington but the order was countermanded until next morning.

Friday March 25, 1864

Drew rations and left the barracks for the depot at 8AM, but did not leave until 3PM, rode in stock cars. Arrived in Columbus at 10PM. Went to the barracks and stayed until 4AM. Weather very disagreeable with rain and snow.

Saturday 26

Were ordered out and started. Took the Ohio Central arrived at Bellair, 175 miles from Columbus at 2PM. From there marched to Wheeling, Virginia, distance 6 miles, crossed the Ohio on a suspension bridge and quartered in a prison house for the night.

Sunday, March 27, 1864

Left Wheeling, Virginia at 11AM for Washington, rode all through western Virginia, arrived at Harper's Ferry 4AM. Crossed the river and then into Maryland, from there proceeded to Washington Junction. Distance from Wheeling, Virginia to Washington 400 miles.

Monday 28

Left Washington Junction for Washington 31 miles distant. Arrived here at 8AM and then went to the barracks and staid until 2PM. We were then ordered to this place. Marched through the City of Washington, and on my way here met one of my old acquaintances.

Tuesday, March 29, 1864

Weather very cold today. Drew clothing and articles for our comfort. Went to the hospital and had an interview (note: interview here refers to conversation) with L.B. Dickerson and ate dinner with him which consisted of eggs, bread and milk.

Wednesday 30

Today weather very disagreeable and cold did not do anything of any importance. Wrote one letter and spent the rest of the time in reading and spending the time as best we could.

Thursday, March 31, 1864

Weather very pleasant today and drew our canteens and rucksacks preparatory to a march and also had a drill from which I was excused on *the account of my wound. In the evening I was visited by L.B. Dickerson from the Carver Hospital* **(see figure 17).**

Friday, April 1

Weather very pleasant and warm, nothing of any importance transpired today. Had drill in the forenoon, did not have any in the afternoon owing to the rain.

<u>Saturday, April 2, 1864</u>

Weather very disagreeable with snow and rain, did not have any duty to perform; only issuing our arms and accoutrements to us. Our arms are imported ones of English manufacture.

Sunday 3

Weather very pleasant and consequently we were on inspection. In the forenoon and afternoon spent the time in reading. At 6PM went on dress parade. Tonight another Company came in from Camp Dennison.

<u>Monday, April 4, 1864</u>

This morning reported to the doctor and at 10AM had Company drill. This afternoon drill was postponed on account of rain. We were examined and all those who were not fit for duty were thrown out. Had a visitor this afternoon and had a very good visit while the rain beat on the roofs.

Tuesday 5

Weather very disagreeable with much rain, had no duty to perform and in the afternoon paid a visit to L.B. Had a good time, got several Portage Democrat newspapers which afforded me some goodly reading matter.

Wednesday, April 6, 1864

Weather very pleasant, had 2 hours of drill and also done my washing. At 6PM had dress parade. Wrote one letter, the balance of the time spent in reading. Today we had orders to leave but the orders were countermanded and we wait for further orders.

Thursday 7

Forenoon we did not have any drill as we were allowed it for washing. Wrote one letter, afternoon was excused from drill. Today another Company came in from Cincinnati. Dress parade at 6PM, weather very pleasant and warm.

Friday, April 8, 1864

Today weather very fine, did not have any drill, in the forenoon and afternoon had an hour's drill. We received marching orders but it was counter-manded. Our destination was Alexandria, Virginia. Dress parade at 6 1/2 as usual. Today another member of the Company was taken to the Pest House with the Smallpox.

Saturday 9

Today went to the city in company with a friend. Visited the Smithsonian Institute and saw some of the greatest curiosities in the world. Returned to camp at 3PM and then got marching orders. We were taken to the city near the Capitol.

Sunday, April 10, 1864

Today spent the first in Capitol Hill Barracks, in front of the Capitol. Went on inspection at 10AM, at 11AM went to church at 4PM had dress parade. Wrote to the Colonel for a transfer to the regiment.

Monday 11

Today went on guard at the Capitol Guard house and in front of the Smithsonian Institute. Our employment being to guard prisoners, mostly the men of our own Army. Weather very pleasant.

Tuesday, April 12, 1864

Today was relieved of guard and reported back to camp. Today great excitement prevails in Congress owing to two members being expelled from the House. Dress parade at 4PM as usual. Weather very fine and warm which makes it quite agreeable standing guard.

Wednesday 13

Was detailed as Depot guard and I was appointed Sergeant of the Guard and was placed in very comfortable quarters. Weather very pleasant, nothing of any importance transpired today, only the same old activity of transporting troops to the front. Today all went quiet in the Senate Chamber.

Thursday, April 14, 1864

Spent the day in lying around the quarters and amusing ourselves as well as we could. Today quite a number of veterans came in. Today for the first time since our arrival at this place received a letter from home.

Friday 15

Today procured a pass to visit the City and a pleasant opportunity of visiting the Senate Chamber and House of Representatives. The Capitol being one of the best specimens of architecture in the world and some of the nicest furniture ever beheld. I also had a good opportunity of seeing the men of both houses and the President's Mansion.

Saturday, April 16, 1864

Today was on guard, weather very disagreeable with rain. Today quite a lot of veterans came on their way to the front. Today was much surprised to learn of the capture of Fort Pillow on the Mississippi River.

Sunday 17

Had inspection at 10AM and then received a pass and went to visit L.B.D., had a very good time. Went to church at 2:30 PM and heard an excellent sermon, then came back to camp and saw several veterans that had just come in. Today weather very fine, at night had a good time reading some periodicals presented by L.B.

Monday, April 18, 1864

Today weather very fine, was on guard and engaged in reading. Nothing of any importance transpired. Veterans came in all the time today. The 10th Jersey came and also 3rd Corp. of VRC. Wrote one letter and received none in return.

Tuesday 19

Today was not on detail and went to camp and done my washing and then returned at 4PM. We moved our quarters to Captain Ripley's. Today nothing of any importance transpired, weather very pleasant and warm. A train has just arrived loaded with veterans.

Wednesday, April 20, 1864

Was Sergeant of the guard at Depot House. Weather very fine and warm to be on duty. Today learned that our troops had met with a disaster in Louisiana. No veterans arrived today. Everything quiet and lively.

Thursday 21

Today was relieved in the forenoon and went to visit the Navy Yard. Had a pleasant trip and in the afternoon went to the Capitol and also to the House of Representatives. Heard the Liquor Law tax discussed and at 3PM went back to quarters and witnessed the arrival of 3 veterans' regiments going to the front. Weather very pleasant and warm.

Friday, April 22, 1864

Today was on guard at Government Depot, weather very pleasant in the forenoon. At 3PM quite a lot of veterans came in. Among the number were two Ohio Cavalry and several boys from Randolph which we were very glad to see. At night wrote a letter. Everything quiet on the front.

Saturday 23

Today was relieved from guard at Depot and reported back to our quarters. In the afternoon, after doing some washing, I went to the House of Representatives and heard several able speakers, then went back to camp and so forth.

Sunday, April 24, 1864

Sunday had inspection as usual in the forenoon. At 11AM went to church, after dinner went to church again in the hospital building. After dinner went to the dress parade and spent the time as best we could.

Monday 25

Was detailed for guard at camp with 15 men. Today Major General Burnside passed through the city with the 9th A.C. comprising, with whites and blacks, 40,000 men, from here went on to Alexandria. Weather very sultry and some rain.

Tuesday, April 26, 1864

Today was relieved from guard and procured a pass and went to Carver Hospital **(see figure 17)**. From there in company with L.B. went to the Patent *office and also to the Gudring* (?) *Hospital and saw J. Andrews formerly of Randolph. While in the town saw many curiosities worth seeing, then went to camp.*

Wednesday 27

Today was detailed for guard around camp, weather very disagreeable and cold owing to the high wind from the river. Nothing of any importance transpired worth mentioning. Today our time was occupied in reading a book entitled "Young Men's Guide". Today wrote one letter.

Thursday, April 28, 1864

Today was relieved from guard. Forenoon done my washing and mending. Afternoon went to the Capitol in company with another gentleman, had quite a good time. Heard the debate on a bill providing for the raising of the revenue bill. Weather very cool owing to the winds from the Potomac. At 3PM received orders to march.

Friday 29

Today after partaking of a breakfast of pork and bread we were marched to the Soldiers Rest **(see figure 18)** *near the Depot and here waiting orders today. Several regiments left Alexandria for the front which had been lying here sometime but whose time is now expired for active duty. Today weather very fine and warm.*

Saturday, April 30, 1864

Today, after partaking of a hearty breakfast, we were marched about one mile from camp to clean our camping ground and after having quite a good time policing were sent back to dinner. Weather very bad with some rain. Just at end an order came for my transfer to my regiment.

Sunday, May 1

Sunday inspection as usual at 3 1/2, weather very cold and disagreeable for the time of year. Our camp is very nicely located in sight of Fort Ellsworth and a short distance from Alexandria. We had a good time of seeing troops going and coming from the front. Today was deprived of the pleasure of going to church.

Monday, May 2, 1864

Today had nothing of any importance to perform, weather very cold and a very heavy tide. Just at evening experienced a very severe storm blowing great quantities of sand which resulted in great inconvenience to us and our shelter tents. Very sudden changes are experienced here.

Tuesday 3

Today the weather very cool. This morning we had quite a lot of fish which were washed up by the tide. Great adversity prevails here at this time; troops are constantly going to the front. Today we received our order to report for examination for our regiment - 20 men were detached today for train guard.

Wednesday, May 4, 1864

Today nothing of any importance transpired. With the exception of a railroad accident in which

2 of our regiment were severely wounded with an amputation of a leg. Weather very cool, tide not as high as usual. Great excitement on the front last night.

Thursday 5

Weather very fine and warm, forenoon had nothing to do of any importance. Afternoon after drilling a squad, wrote a letter home. Today we learned that fighting is going on at front. Several went out on train guard for the purpose of bringing in wounded men of which there were many. Nights very cool and disagreeable.

Friday, May 6, 1864

Today weather very fine, forenoon went to the river fishing, afternoon had an examination and was pronounced fit for duty. Today nothing was heard from the front only that our men were advancing. Everything has been suspended and the rolling stock ordered to the war.

Saturday 7

Received a pass to go to the city of Washington. Took the boat at 10AM, and after arriving in the city went to Carver Hospital. Had a very good visit, from there went to the city and had a negative taken. After having a good time went back and also learned of the victory of our army near Chancellorsville.

Sunday, May 8, 1864

Today had inspection as usual at 8AM. The rest of the time spent in the cemetery in front of camp.

Weather very fine but extremely hot; even so much to make it uncomfortable. We learned the glad news today that our troops had gained a decisive victory over the Rebs.

Monday 9

Today weather very warm and sultry, forenoon had drill; afternoon went fishing but met with no success. We also learned of the great victory of our arms on the Rapidan. With such news we feel cheerful and realize that soon we will be with the loved ones of our lives.

Tuesday, May 10, 1864

Weather very fine but extremely warm. Forenoon had drill afternoon nothing of any importance transpired. Tonight we learned of the success of General Grant, it caused great excitement in camp. With such men we need not entertain any fears of the result. Heavy firing from Fort Ellsworth near this camp.

Wednesday 11

Today weather very warm and some rain, forenoon had company drill, afternoon drill as usual. Wrote one letter to my original company, also learned of the expected success of our arms in Virginia. Just at evening we had a very large mail but unfortunately did not get any letters.

Thursday, May 12, 1864

Weather very rainy today. Several companies left and I was obliged to go on guard, had a very wet time of it. Today we learn very cheery news from the front and indications are we will soon be victorious.

Friday 13

Today was relieved from guard and was very glad owing to this storm. Several companies left for Fredericksburg and we also had orders to be ready. Today we have cheering news from the Potomac. With such news we live with great hopes.

Saturday, May 14, 1864

Today I was detailed to take charge of a fatigue squad until noon, after noon trained considerably. Today we came in receipt of quite cheering news from the front to the effect that U.S. had made another victorious battle.

Sunday 15

Sunday morning had inspection as usual at 8AM and then went to church and heard one of the ablest sermons I ever heard from the pulpit and also saw Bishop Asbury. Weather very stormy and rain this afternoon, wrote one letter.

Monday, May 16, 1864

Weather very warm, forenoon went on drill. Today nothing of any importance transpired, for dinner had a mess of fish. Received quite a supply of Christian Mission stories which was very interesting to the mind.

Tuesday 17

Today nothing of any importance transpired, weather very fine, forenoon had drill. The remainder of the time spent on reading. Afternoon received three letters.

Wednesday, May 18, 1864

Weather very fine with some rain, forenoon had drill, afternoon spent with distinguished gentlemen, had a grand time, and also wrote two letters. And everything passes quite well and indications are that we will soon out-weather the gale of soldiering.

Thursday 19

Today went out as train guard on or near the old Bull Run Battleground. Arrived at camp about 1PM, ate dinner and spent the afternoon on reading and sleep. Today is very pleasant and made us feel somewhat lazy owing to the hot sun, a very bad disease wherever found.

Friday, May 20, 1864

Today procured a pass and went to the City of Washington and had a splendid visit with L.B., ate dinner with Herbert Snyder. After dinner went to the city after seeing friends. Started for Alexandria, arrived in camp about dark. Weather very fine and extremely warm. Went to the city on the (?).

Saturday 21

Today nothing of any importance, forenoon wrote a letter, afternoon in reading and other amusements. Weather very fine but extremely hot.

Sunday, May 22, 1864

Was detailed for camp guard at 9 o'clock, had company inspection as usual. Did not get the chance to go to church today. This afternoon had a very severe storm of thunder and lightning. Today was one of great discouragement as I could not attend church. Went to the soldiers burying ground where there are interred 1,875 soldiers who died in the hospitals in & around this city. Among the number is several of the 76th V.I.

Fort Ethan Allen mounts 32 guns. Among the forts of this most formidable characteristics are Fort Ellsworth, Lyon, Mercer & Geary.

Monday 23

Today was relieved from guard at 9AM. Forenoon part of the company was detailed to go to the Soldiers Rest on guard. Received a letter from home today and found everything in the best of circumstances. Weather very pleasant and agree-able, had dress parade at 3PM.

Tuesday, May 24, 1864

Nothing of any importance transpired had drill as usual, wrote a letter home. Just at night we had a severe storm. News not very encouraging from the front.

Wednesday 25

Today was busy between times in cleaning my accoutrements, afternoon had drill. Weather very *warm, suffered considerable from my wound. News good from the front. Tonight it stormed quite hard.*

Thursday, May 26, 1864

Weather very stormy and consequently nothing of any importance transpired. Suffered somewhat from my wound today owing to the dampness of the weather. Today quite a number of soldiers were interred in the cemetery near this place.

Friday 27

Was detailed for guard went as a guard to a wood train after proceeding 12 miles I was stationed with 25 men to guard a bridge but we did not have chance to give Mosby (note: rebel Col. Mosby's Raiders) *a reception as was desired by all. Arrived in camp about 2PM, all quiet, no interesting news from the front; weather pleasant.*

Saturday, May 28, 1864

Weather very fine nothing of any importance transpired. Suffered somewhat from my wound, wrote one letter today.

Sunday 29

Today did not go on duty, reported to the doctor. Weather very fine nothing transpired today of any importance. Today was deprived of going to church and spent time on reading & writing.

Monday, May 30, 1864

Weather very fine, morning went to the doctors and passed an examination. Several returned from furlough today who had reenlisted. Nothing of any importance transpired, very encouraging news from the front. Busied ourselves in reading and writing.

Tuesday 31

Was detailed for camp guard, had a very pleasant time near the cemetery watched the internment of several soldiers. Weather very warm at night, received a letter from home.

Wednesday, June 1, 1864

Today was relieved from guard at 9AM and then reported to the doctor for examination. Forenoon spent in sleep mostly, weather very warm & sultry. News very encouraging from the front, wrote a letter home today, etc., etc., etc.

Thursday 2

Weather very pleasant, reported to the doctor and wrote several letters, otherwise nothing of any importance transpired, news cheering from the front. Just at eve received orders to break up the detachment and report to our respective regiments.

Friday, June 3, 1864

Packed our knapsacks at an early hour. At 10 o'clock, started for the city took the cars at Alexandria arrived in Washington about 2PM in the same old quarters to the great dissatisfaction of the men owing to the varmints in the old buildings. Weather very pleasant and cool.

Saturday 4

Today procured a pass and went to the city and had an excellent visit with L. B Dickenson at the Carver Hospital. From there went to camp and then went to bed as I was very tired. Weather very fine and cheering news from the front.

Sunday, June 5, 1864

Detailed for guard at headquarters and consequently did not get to church as was my desire. Weather very warm & sultry, nothing of any importance transpired. News good from the front. Today a man was obliged to carry a barrel for disobedience of orders.

Monday 6

Today was relieved from guard at 8 ½. Returned to camp forenoon and cleaned my gun. At night a severe storm came up and consequently we did not have any dress parade. No news from the front today. An election was held for Mayor candidates Wallach & Sims.

Tuesday, June 7, 1864

Went on guard at Camp Baker 19 miles from camp near the Lincoln Hospital **(see figure 19)**, *where they're now constructing a hospital. Afternoon drew clothing; nothing of any importance transpired today, weather very fine.*

June 8

Was relieved from guard, came to camp and signed the payroll's property to receiving pay.

Weather very fine, wrote a letter today and spent the remainder of the time in reading & writing.

Thursday, June 9, 1864

Went on guard at headquarters, had a splendid time with the exception of several drunken men. Nothing of any importance transpired, did receive our pay which consisted of $26.

Friday 10

Relieved from guard and went to the city and sent money home. By (?) (?). From there went to the Soldiers Library and got a book entitled "History of England". From there went to the jewelry store and bought a pen and then returned to camp, Weather very fine.

Saturday, June 11, 1864

Today was detailed for guard at Camp Baker. Had a splendid time and then, while not on duty, wrote a letter so we passed the time. Received a letter from home today and also some papers. Nothing of any importance transpired today, weather very fine and agreeable.

Sunday 12

Was relieved from guard and went to quarters. Wrote a letter and spent the remainder of the time visiting and writing. Weather very fine, nothing of any importance transpired, going to church this afternoon if nothing happens.

Monday, June 13, 1864

Today was detailed for guard at camp, had a good time. Nothing of any importance transpired today. In the evening went to a restaurant and had a good dish of ice cream.

Tuesday 14

Procured a pass and went to Ft. Ethan Allen on the Virginia side. Had a good visit with Lewis Kirk of Co. VI 109 6VG (?), after staying until 3PM returned to the city after a walk of 7 miles which fatigued me very much. Weather very fine and extremely warm.

Wednesday, June 15, 1864

Detailed to go to Camp Baker on guard about one mile from quarters, had a good time, weather very fine. At night witnessed the fireworks which consisted of balloons and skyrockets which lighted up the heavens very much.

Thursday 16

Relieved from guard, went to camp and then prepared ourselves for General Inspection which comes once every month. Today news cheering from the front. Weather very warm, received a net gram (?) Billy Rymers.

Friday, June 17, 1864

Detailed for Quartermaster guard, had a good time, relieved at 4PM and went to camp and wrote a letter. Today we had good news from the front which indicates a speedy fall of the stronghold. Weather very fine and warm.

Saturday 18

Today was relieved from guard and then spent the time in (?). About noon got orders to go to our regiment. Afternoon busy in getting ready to go, weather very fine and warm.

Sunday, June 19, 1864

Returned from Carver Hospital this morning after having a good visit. At 9AM started for Camp Distribution in VA, arrived about 2PM. It is situated on a fine piece of ground and well constructed (?) to make a soldier comfortable. Wrote 2 letters today.

Monday 20

Spent the first day in camp very lonesome. Excessive heat at night. Went to Meeting and had a good time

Tuesday, June 21, 1864

Nothing of any importance transpired today, with the exception of some men that came in. Weather very warm and disagreeable. Was very unlucky last night having pocketbook and money taken.

Wednesday 22

Today was on Fatigue Squad or a shoveling squad. Today quite a number of men left for the Front and several came in from Fort Henry. Last evening went to the Temperance Tent and had a very excellent time.

Thursday, June 23, 1864

Spent the time in reading, nothing of any importance transpired today. Several recruits came in and sent for the Western Army. Weather very warm.

Friday 24

At 9AM went to church, had a good time. Quite a number of men came in today for the Western Army. Weather the warmest of the year, it being too hot to do anything. At night went to church.

Saturday, June 25, 1864

Weather very warm, almost too hot to live. Nothing of any interest transpired today. Several came in, some which joined our squad for the West. At night went to church.

Sunday 26

Meeting at 9AM and preaching at 10 ½ by Fisher. Afternoon went to Chapel and wrote a letter. At night went to church again, but it was very uncomfortable owing to the heat.

Monday June, 27, 1864

Today went to Church after witnessing the departure of about 900 men for the Army of the Potomac. Afternoon had quite a nice swim which made it much cooler. At night went to church and had a nice time. This evening received orders to leave tomorrow...

Tuesday 28

Left Camp Distribution at 9AM then marched to Washington a distance of 6 miles. Went to the Baltic Depot and camped there for the night and then left for Columbus after some time to go to the Camp and get some necessary articles.

Wednesday, June 29, 1864

Rode all day on the cars of the Baltic & Ohio passing through Harpers Ferry. In the morning arrived opposite Bellaire at 6PM crossed the river and immediately took the cars for Columbus arrived at that place at 2AM and went to the barracks.

Thursday 30

Lay in camp but had quite a good time visiting with some of my old friends. We experienced a very fine shower today which made everything look nice. At 8PM left for Cincinnati after having no sleep for 3 nights.

Friday, July 1, 1864

Arrived in Cincinnati about 6AM, from there went to the Michael Barracks one of the most miserable places in the known world. Remained closed up all day without provision to go out at all. Weather very warm. Today suffered severely from a finger supposed to be broken.

Saturday 2

Left Cincinnati at 9AM enroute for Louisville took the boat called General Buell. Arrived in

Louisville about 12PM after having a very pleasant trip. The trip was made pleasant by appearances of many (?) (?) of the Hoosier state.

Sunday, July 3, 1864

Left the boat at 6AM marched to the City Barracks after being there awhile I was examined and sent to the hospital arrived there at 10 ½ AM, No. 7 Hospital located near the Nashville Depot and in sight of Jeffersonville, Ind.

Monday 4

In hospital, the 4th was spent by no great enjoyment on our part only a good dinner prepared by the ladies of the City. Louisville was thronged by (?) to the celebration 4 miles from this place. Weather very pleasant but very warm.

Tuesday, July 5, 1864

Today spent in hospital suffered some what with pain in head. Nothing of any importance transpired today with the exception of a large lot of wounded men that came in this morning from the front. Weather very pleasant.

Wednesday 6

Today after procuring a pass I went to visit Lieutenant Booth of Co. D 104 and stayed until noon and then went to hospital. Nothing of any importance transpired today. Tonight learned of the capture of Petersburg.

Thursday, July 7, 1864

Today at my request was discharged from hospital and went to Exchange Barracks. Arrived there at 8AM, nothing of any importance transpired today. Several started out today enroute for the front.

Friday 8

Today remained yet in barracks No. 1. At 9AM procured a pass & went to (?) Hospital to visit some of the 104 regiment that were there, did not find any of them, from there went back. Expecting to leave at 5PM for Nashville but was disappointed. Weather very fine.

Saturday, July 9, 1864

Today remained in barracks, was expected to leave but was disappointed. Spent the day very lonesome, nothing occurred of interest. Several came in today for the front, the number was several for my Division 3rd Corp.

Sunday 10

Left Louisville enroute for Nashville at 8AM rode in second class cars and arrived in Nashville at 5PM after a long ride of 195 miles. On our arrival were escorted to the military prison for the night, met several wounded men in there.

Monday, July 11, 1864

Today left Nashville for Chattanooga at 8AM. Had a very unpleasant trip, in box cars, the ride being very rough. Arrived at Stephenson, AL at

11AM, stayed overnight. It was very pleasant to see the nice fields of grain.

Tuesday 12

Left Stephenson for Chattanooga at 9AM arrived in sight of Lookout Mountain. Arrived at Chattanooga at 11AM and went to the Soldiers Home from there went to Convalescent Camp about 1 mile from town. Encamped in big tents and cooked our own grub.

Wednesday, July 13, 1864

Spent in convalescent camp, forenoon built a cabin, afternoon was detailed to go to the Depot as fatigue squad, remained there all night.

Thursday 14

Today after having breakfast went to the Christian Commission (Note: the Christian Commission was on the order of the USO) *and wrote several letters from there went to camp again. Today quite a number of men went to the front. Today had quite a good conversation with one of the 102nd Connecticut while at the Commission.*

Friday July 15, 1864

This morning after having breakfast went to the Christian Commission and wrote a letter. Came back and had a good dish of beans for dinner. This afternoon quite a large squad went to the front as a wagon guard. Weather very warm.

Saturday 16

After having breakfast went to the Christian Commission and procured some good reading material. Just before sunset in company with 2 other gentlemen went to see the 14 OSC troops on dress parade.

Sunday, July 17, 1864

Today was detailed for guard in camp after posting my relief went to church and heard a very able discourse from the Sgt of the Christian Commission. Today an order came for all 23rd Corps. convalescents to report to their commands.

Monday 18

Relieved from guard & procured a pass and went to town & learned that Trent Robinson was there. Afternoon returned to camp and at night received an order for all of the 23rd Corp to go to their regiments that were fit for duty.

Tuesday, July 19, 1864

This morning went to the Commission & procured some reading material. Today suffered severely from a bad cold. Today the Convalescents of the 23rd went to the front, one of Co. E went. Weather very warm and sultry.

Wednesday 20

Forenoon went to the city, afternoon lay in camp. Today 2,000 left for the front as cattle guard. Had a fine shower which aided very much to relieve us from the heat.

Thursday, July 21, 1864

This morning went out on a trading trip, got some potatoes and had a fine dinner of ham and new potatoes. Nothing transpired today worth-while, the same old camp scenes. As we stand in camp we can see darkies busy fortifying a hill in front of camp.

Friday 22

Forenoon went to the city and wrote a letter. Afternoon everything was alive with excitement over the capture of Atlanta, flags hung in & over all prominent buildings. At night went to church in the old building used by people of former days.

Saturday, July 23, 1864

Today was quite unwell and consequently re-mained close in camp. This morning met one of Co. II boys that had just come from the rear, had a quite a good interview with him. Weather very warm and sultry, potatoes for breakfast.

Sunday 24

This forenoon spent in camp & Christian Com-mission. Afternoon went to the Depot and saw several wounded men that had just came in from the front. Quite a number of men went from this place to the front; among the number was one of Co. II. At night went to Church.

Monday, July 25, 1864

Nothing of any importance transpired with the exception of encouraging news from the front. In the evening of yesterday the body of General McPherson arrived under an escort of officers and was taken to Stedman's headquarters. Today had a mess of string beans for dinner.

Tuesday 26

Morning spent on reading, afternoon went to the Depot and saw several wounded that had just come in from the front, some hard looking wounded. At night went to church, had a good time, Christian Commission Sgt. preached.

Wednesday, July 27, 1864

Forenoon remained in camp and went to the Commission, expecting a letter but was disappointed. Had a very fine shower which added very much to cool the air at night. Went to prayer meeting which lasted until 11PM.

Thursday 28

Today nothing of any importance, several regiments came in from the front that their time had expired, among the number was the II OVA. We learned glorious news from the front today which makes everyone look cheerful.

Friday, July 29, 1864

Went to town and procured reading matter at Commission. Nothing of any importance transpired, several came in from the Rear. At night went to church, had a glorious meeting.

Saturday 30

This morning drew clothing after that there came an order for examination of the camp by the Surgeons and inspections made as they saw fit. Tonight go to church had a conference meeting of which we expect to realize great benefit from.

Sunday, July 31, 1864

This morning went to church at 10 1/2 AM, had an excellent time. Forenoon spent in camp. Nothing of any importance transpired everything quiet as though no war was near. Evening was here and at night had a good meeting.

Monday, August 1

Got breakfast and went to town for mail but was disappointed. We got good news from the front. Today some 200 wounded came in morning on it 20 from front of Freenter (?).

Tuesday, August 2, 1864

Spent in camp most of the time, nothing of any interest with the exception of a good dish of beans for dinner. At night went to church had an excellent time, enjoyed it very much. About 300 wounded arrived from the front today.

Wednesday 3

Forenoon spent in camp, afternoon went to the city and was caught in a very severe storm but by evening arrived in camp before the rain and then wrote two letters. While the gentle rains patter on the roof and on leaves we recall the fond and cherished memories of the past.

Thursday, August 4, 1864

Today nothing of any importance transpired with the exception of an examination of all men not fit for the front. Afternoon had a very severe storm, at night went to church.

Friday 5

This morning ordered to go to Nashville at 12AM, left camp in the AM (?) went to depot but did not get away until 5PM, rode in hospital cars.

Saturday, August 6, 1864

Arrived in Nashville at 1 o'clock. PM remained til 3 at depot. Were then taken to No. 1 Hospital in the eastern part of town, most of the wounded taken to No. 2 **(see figure 20)**.

104th OVI was engaged in a (?). Atlanta captured Sept. 3rd 1864 caused by a flank movement as the right of the advance led by the 23rd Corps.

Sunday 7

Spent the first day in Nashville, enjoyed it very much but without the privilege of attending church. Everything a result of will. Plenty of good books to read_and keep our interest.

Sunday saw the body of Capt. Allison a g?????? chief killed 7 1/2 miles from this city by a private of Duke's cavalry firing 3 balls through his head.

Monday, August 8, 1864

Today was one of great lonesomeness, nothing of any interest or employ, was in bed with reading matter. Quite a number left for the front.

Tuesday 9

Forenoon spent most of time in reading and writing, occasionally looking out the window and getting a view of the city and the splendid buildings. The building now used as a hospital was formerly the Female Seminary Building.

Wednesday, August 10, 1864

Spent in hospital, nothing of any interest occurred, wrote some letters. This evening one of our number was called away with disease fever. Sadly and earnestly we feel the importance of preparation when we look on the reasons of lifeless men and are sad to think what will I profit to gain the whole world and lose the Lord.

Thursday 11

Today nothing of any importance transpired, wrote a letter and spent the time as usual in reading and chatting on the prospects of the war. Very pleasant day with showers at intervals.

Friday, August 12, 1864

Forenoon I did not get out much, suffered somewhat from wound. Just before noon had a great treat of melon which we relished very much. Had some fine showers today which made us feel like young ducks.

Saturday 13

Spent in hospital, nothing of any importance transpired. Fortunately the… (Faded and unreadable)

Sunday, August 14, 1864

Most of the day spent in hospital in reading and at night went to church of Presbyterian denomination **(see figure 21)**. (The rest unreadable, looks like his pen was running out of ink)

Monday 15

Forenoon went to the State agent and procured some writing material. Afternoon spent in hospital as it was very rainy at dusk. Received a letter from a friend for the first time since June.

Tuesday, August 16, 1864

Today remained in camp or hospital as we were expecting an examination. I learned that my regiment had been engaged and suffered severe losses, 1 killed and many wounded. Weather very warm, suffered a good deal from my wound today. 23rd Corps, 1st Brigade, 3rd Division made an unsuccessful charge losing about 400 men. Wounded of Co. II: Dole, Charles, (?), *Ford, Camble, Ferry,* (?).

Wednesday 17

This morning had general examination but I did not do very well. Several sent to the front, nothing else occurred of any interest. Wrote a letter home today, but received none. Weather very rainy and disagreeable.

Thursday, August 18, 1864

Didn't get out much today as it was too wet and suffered somewhat from the wound. Had a fine treat of watermelon from the Christian Commission;

efforts which are relished very much in the stormy weather. Nothing from the front worth mentioning.

Friday 19
Today spent in the hospital nothing of any importance transpired with the exception of a general clearing sky and consequently I lit out and went to the city. Weather very rainy and disagreeable.

Saturday, August 20, 1864
The same old amusement is again resumed, reading and study good books of which we have a good supply. Most useful ones such as; Baxter's Works, Hall's Scripture History etc. No patients admitted today, nothing transpired.

Sunday 21
Spent in hospital reading, did not get to meeting as inspection interfered with. At night went to church and heard an excellent sermon from text; "what is this that thou hast done?"

Monday, August 22, 1864
Very pleasant, no rain. Had a general move today which resulted in changing me to near and among wounded men.

Tuesday 23
Today spent in ward and nothing of any importance transpired, several went to the front. Learned from the doctor today that everything looks well. Took a walk over part of the city and had a view of the Cumberland River.

Wednesday, August 24, 1864

Today went on duty (illegible) liked it very well. Got very tired for the 1st day. No new patients admitted of any account, wrote a letter home.

Thursday 25

On duty as usual, kept pretty busy most of the time in satisfying the many wants of the sick. We love good news from the front. Nothing occurred in hospital of any interest, several men operated on since yesterday.

Friday, August 26, 1864

Attending to the wants of the wounded as usual, which made me very tired by night. Wrote letter to attorney.

Saturday 27

Today busy engaged in cleaning my arms preparing for inspection. In afternoon had a rest of a couple of hours and wrote some letters for men in the ward. No letters from home, somewhat discouraged for that reason.

Sunday, August 28, 1864

This morning after doing our normal work had inspection as usual. At night went to church and heard an excellent sermon.

Monday 29

Nothing of any interest occurred. In the afternoon went to town to look up some of the 104th 6VRG, did not find any. Today another man died from wound.

Tuesday, August 30, 1864

Nothing of any importance transpired, on duty as usual. At night went to Prayer Meeting in the Chapel, heard one of the best sermons (he goes on to quote part of the Bible verse, however, it is illegible).

Wednesday 31

Forenoon on duty, afternoon went to town and procured a watermelon and it was a fine treat! Today the city was thrown into alarm by the reported approach of Wheeler's Raiders, but it turned out to be a canard.

Thursday, September 1, 1864

Everything is wild with excitement on report of Wheeler's approach to the city. Last night we were all called out in line of battle but it turned out to be of no use as no Rebs came in sight.

Friday 2

This morning after getting breakfast we were again called out in line and stacked arms and was lying under orders all day but Wheeler didn't come. Wrote two letters in the meantime, one to the front. Weather very warm and disagreeable.

Saturday, September 3, 1864

This day was one of unusual excitement on account of the great victory of our arms and in spite of Wheeler's operations everyone was jubilant. This afternoon 100 guns were fired from Fort Negley (note: fort has been restored) and surrounding ones which sounded like thunder and added much to the enthusiasm of the people.

Sunday 4

This morning went at scrubbing as usual for inspection, but it did not come. At night went to church and heard an excellent discourse on our very sick. Saw in the midst of a crowd a soldier breathing his last which he'd been carried in by a guard.

Monday, September 5, 1864

Forenoon busy in cleaning up etc. Nothing of any importance transpired worth mentioning except the great rejoicing over the victory in Atlanta. Afternoon went to the city and state agency.

Tuesday 6

Forenoon busy cleaning up and eating. Afternoon went to town and learned of the sudden death of John Morgan (note: of Morgan's Raiders). How the people should rejoice that he who has done such an amount of mischief is gone. No penitentiary now shuts him out of the world but he who will (illegible)

Wednesday, September 7, 1864

Forenoon busy scrubbing until nearly noon, afternoon wrote a letter. Everything wild with excitement over the great news. We may soon expect to hear serious news from our brave boys who compose our armies. (Rest illegible)

Thursday 8

Forenoon spent on duty, afternoon went to the city with a friend and procured a treat of melon and peaches. At night went out on a walk, had a pleasant time. Everything so cheerful over the news from Sherman.

Friday, September 9, 1864

Spent in our usual occupations and reading, at night went to prayer meeting, enjoyed one of the best season of communion with (?) ever experienced, broke up with shaking of hands.

Saturday 10

Forenoon spent partly in reading and afternoon went to town and saw several recruits that had just come in enroute for the front. At night went in camp with a friend and spent the evening on a pleasant walk.

Sunday, September 11, 1864

This morning kept busy in preparing for inspection. At 10AM went to church and heard an excellent discourse from our post chaplain. At night also went to church at the Methodist church and heard the best sermon of my life portraying heaven in all its splendor and enjoyments.

Monday 12

Today busy as usual, about noon the unusual quietude of the city was broken by the booming of cannons in honor of the recent victory. Spent part of the day in reading The Life of Payson, at night *went to the State House and heard several good speeches.*

Great commotions in honor of recent victories, every house of note being lighted up at night. Went to State House **(see figure 22)** *and heard speeches from Col. Bird and Col. Crawford. Members of the House Committee were chosen to draft resolutions for the soldiers and people of the North desiring to denounce any party that are now in favor of compromise with traitors of their own army. Gov. Johnson's* (note: the soon to be VP Andrew Johnson) *address was one of true interest being the conditions of our country plainly before our eyes and the necessity of a codicil* (?) *suffered by contributions of many of men. At the conclusion cheers were great.* (The rest is illegible)

<u>Tuesday, September 13, 1864</u>

Nothing of any importance transpired, busy in cleaning. At night went to church and had a good time. Tonight another of our number has died and gone to rest.

Wednesday 14

Forenoon spent most of the time in reading Baxter's Life, which afforded me great comfort. At night went to church and had a good time. Night very cool which made me want some hot meals. Another man died tonight.

Thursday, September 15, 1864

Forenoon went to town and wrote a letter home. Afternoon staid in the hospital expecting to get our pay but failed. Weather very cool particularly at night which is a common thing in this clime. No news of any interest today, all quiet in Nashville.

Friday 16

Nothing of any importance transpired, at night went to class meeting. Expected to get pay but did not get any.

Saturday, September 17, 1864

Today busy cleaning my arms and preparing for inspection on the morrow. At night, in company with a friend took a walk and had a good time. Got 3 letters today which added greatly to cheer up our minds.

Sunday 18

Went to church in the forenoon to the (?) Methodist Church had a good time. At night also went to church and listened to an excellent discourse from a Lt. Cole of the Army.

Monday, September 19, 1864

Today wrote a letter and received 2 which pleased me very much, particularly to hear the folks at home were well. Afternoon expected our pay but were foiled, nothing of any import transpired. One more soldier died last night leaving a family to mourn his loss.

Tuesday 20

Forenoon busy cleaning up, afternoon went to church and also at night. When we returned the door was locked and we felt the fruits of going to church had to be our dorm.

Wednesday, September 21, 1864

This morning went to Branch and found 2 men of my Co. wounded and had a good interview with them. Afternoon had an examination but I escaped by going to town. Am getting along fine, not much to do but lots of fun and good books to read.

Thursday 22

Nothing of any interest occurred, busy at work as usual. Afternoon went to town and also to the Christian Commission. Learned of the great victory of Sheridan over the Rebs which produced great excitement in the hospital.

Friday, September 23, 1864

Forenoon went visiting and had a good visit. Afternoon went to town in company with a friend, at night witnessed awful scene, saw a poor soldier bleed to death and while dying the nurse could be seen with his finger over the artery trying to keep him alive.

Saturday 24

Forenoon received our pay of $32. Afternoon went to town and procured some necessary articles. At 3PM went to church and had a good meeting, at night wrote a letter, weather very cold.

Sunday, September 25, 1864

Forenoon had inspection, at 10 ½ went to church and also at night. Spent the day to a good advantage in reading and writing, weather quite cool. Sermon from 2nd chapter of John 4th verse "will then be made whole".

Monday 26

Forenoon went to visit some of my cohorts, had a good visit. Afternoon went to town and procured articles for the boys. Nothing of any interest occurred. News from the front energizing, morale very high, weather pleasant.

Tuesday, September 27, 1864

Forenoon spent in hospital reading & writing. Afternoon went to town with a friend. Tonight Johnson speaks in the State house and also a torchlight procession of the Oddfellows.

Wednesday 28

Forenoon spent in hospital and visiting at #1, afternoon staid in hospital. Today heard news of the raid of Forrest (note: Confederate Gen'l Nathaniel Bedford Forrest) *on the railroad. Received no mail today.*

Thursday, September 29, 1864

Forenoon spent in hospital, afternoon went to Division 2 and had a great time. Suffered somewhat from my wound owing to the stormy weather. Tonight wrote a letter to Washington City and also received one from there, news good.

Friday 30

Forenoon went out on visit; forenoon changed my employment to that of cooking. At night staid in hospital as it rained to prevent me from going to church. Night quite cold and dreary, news good from the front.

Saturday, October 1, 1864

Today began cooking (?) and overseeing things done. Afternoon spent in writing letter & at night in house, nothing going on of any interest.

Sunday 2

Forenoon spent in cleaning up as usual, afternoon could not get to attend church, went at night to church and heard an excellent sermon from "What will I do to be saved?" delivered by an Army Chaplain.

Monday, October 3, 1864

Forenoon spent in house, afternoon went to the Gallery and procured some pictures. Nothing of interest transpired today with the exception of some new troops coming in. At night spent in reading & writing.

Tuesday 4

Forenoon went to town and procured some necessary articles. Afternoon spent in hospital in reading and writing. Tonight very stormy and cold, several went to the front today.

Wednesday, October 5, 1864

Forenoon spent in hospital, afternoon went to town. Weather very stormy with much rain. At night read from a book entitled "Clerical Memoirs".

Thursday 6

Forenoon drew clothing and went to town. Afternoon spent in reading & sewing. Weather very pleasant and warm. Saw several new recruits going through, news good and encouraging. Tonight spent in hospital in cooking & (?).

Friday, October 7, 1864

Today spent in hospital, about noon the second (?) caught fire but done little damage. At night went to the State House where arrangements were made voting a committee which was appointed to open parks (pools?) at each hospital serving the worst of all Ohio soldiers (??)

Saturday 8

Forenoon spent in hospital, afternoon went to town and had a good time. At night spent in hospital reading & writing. Weather very cold and disagreeable, news from the front good with favorable results.

Sunday, October 9, 1864

Forenoon spent in hospital and preparing for inspection. Afternoon went to meeting at No. 2 Hospital but on going was disappointed not finding any preacher. At night went to the McKenzie Methodist Church and heard an excellent discourse from Revelations by Chaplain. Tonight suffered *from my wound which bled profusely at times today. Went to the mass meeting for the purpose of making preparedness for the coming election, the chairman being Col. Canby of the 66th Ohio.*

Monday 10

Spent in hospital reading & writing, nothing of any interest occurred. Today remained close to the kitchen as it was very cold and disagreeable. Today was detailed as an attendant. Tonight spent in writing a letter home.

Tuesday, October 11, 1864

Forenoon after doing my morning work went to election and voted for the Old Buckeye State. Afternoon spent in hospital and read from history. Tonight most of the boys went to town but I remained in and read and wrote.

Wednesday 12

Forenoon after performing morning labor had inspection and examination but I being a fortunate one did not have to go. Afternoon went to No. 2 Hospital and had a good time. At night spent in writing to Aunt Mary C (?). *Night very pleasant.*

Thursday, October 13, 1864

Forenoon went to town and also to Christian Commission. Afternoon remained in hospital at reading & writing. Today learned of the great victory of the Republican Party - the vote of the soldiers will greatly increase the vote.

Friday 14

Morning went to No. 2 Hospital, afterwards wrote a letter. Afternoon remained in hospital reading & writing. At night busy reading, weather very cool and disagreeable, but we have come to expect cool weather. Wrote a letter home today.

<u>*Saturday, October 15, 1864*</u>

Forenoon went to Chattanooga Depot **(see figure 23)**, *afternoon remained in hospital and read, it being very rainy and disagreeable. At night after going to bed was aroused by an alarm bell of fire which consumed the convent slaughterhouse.*

Sunday 16

Forenoon busy preparing for inspection did not go to church until night. Heard an excellent discourse from 17th chapter (?). *At 9PM a soldier was brought in dead, shot by a Negro a few yards from the hospital.*

<u>*Monday, October 17, 1864*</u>

Today busy as usual cooking and reading, afternoon went to No. 14 Hospital. Tonight orders came to furlough all injured soldiers for the election from the hospitals. Tonight busy reading from history.

Tuesday 18

Remained in hospital most of the day, at night busy reading & writing. For the first time learned of the great commotion in the Sherman department. Weather very pleasant.

Wednesday, October 19, 1864

Forenoon remained in hospital, nothing of any interest. Several went from the hospital for their regiments, weather very pleasant.

Thursday 20

Forenoon went to town and had a great time. Afternoon spent in hospital cooking, reading etc. Nothing of any interest occurred. Today an order came allowing all Illinois soldiers to go home for voting.

Friday, October 21, 1864

Forenoon was greatly rejoiced over the victory by Sheridan in the valley over Longstreet. Weather very cold and disagreeable, night spent in reading history and wrote a letter home.

Saturday 22

Weather very cold and consequently remained in house all day. Nothing of interest occurred except an order allowing all Michigan soldiers to go home to vote, tonight busy reading.

Sunday, October 23, 1864

Forenoon busy in preparing for inspection, at night listened to an excellent discourse from Chaplain connected to the army, weather very cool.

Monday 24

Monday nothing of interest occurred with the exception of an unusual excitement over Sheridan's victory over Longstreet. At night remained in the hospital and studied arithmetic.

Tuesday, October 25, 1864

Forenoon received a letter from the front the subject being good news. At night an order came allowing all soldiers the privilege of going home to vote. Weather very pleasant, at night a storm came by which resulted in a rainy day Wednesday.

Wednesday 26

Remained in hospital on account of rain. Nothing of interest with the exception of a large addition to the hospital of 40 men from (?). Political excitement very great, anxiously awaiting the contest approaching.

Thursday, October 27, 1864

Weather very wet and cold, nothing of any interest occurred. At night (???).

Friday 28

Today had a general cleaning out of men. Men went home on furlough and also an order came for the (?) Corps. Today busy as usual cooking and reading from history.

Saturday, October 29, 1864

Great excitement today by reason of men going on furlough. Weather very cool, wrote a letter and read from history. Last night a soldier was shot by a Negro.

Sunday 30

No inspection but a general cleaning up. Went to church and heard an excellent sermon from a chaplain in the army. After coming from meeting we received orders for the Ohio soldiers to report for furlough.

Monday, October 31, 1864

Today busy preparing for our journey home. Nothing of interest occurred except the excitement produced by the granting of furlough. News great and encouraging, weather very pleasant and warm.

Tuesday, November 1

An unusual excitement prevailed on account of furloughs. Remained in hospital, at night wrote a letter and read from history. Quite a reduction in numbers today from great news, mostly wounded, to furlough them for the election.

Wednesday, November 2, 1864

Today took charge of cooking department in the absence of the Ohio boys. Weather very rainy and disagreeable, afternoon wrote a letter. Received quite a lot of men from Chattanooga some from 100th Ohio of General (?) brigade.

Thursday 3

This morning all of the furloughed men left, my furlough came but I did not accept as it is for 15 days. Another car of men came in from Chattanooga, was very busy learning men to cook. Weather very pleasant, no rain and must be 80.

Friday, November 4, 1864

This morning up very early for breakfast for men, are always busy all day as our help was all gone. Weather very cool at night, another soldier of the 19th died after suffering of 4 months.

Saturday 5

Remained in hospital all day, at night went to town and witnessed the torchlight procession after a great display & (?) we all rejoiced to the (?) and listened to several speakers, among the number was Judge (?).

Sunday, November 6, 1864

Forenoon remained in hospital until afternoon, went to meeting and had a good meeting. At night did not go as it rained very hard and has for several days which makes it very disagreeable going out.

Monday 7

Nothing of any interest occurred today. Today witnessed an operation on a Rebel. Weather very wet, tonight remained in hospital in company with my partners reading & writing.

Tuesday, November 8, 1864

Forenoon remained in the hospital; afternoon went to the election at 2nd Division which I think will result in the election of Abe. Tonight busy reading from history & tinkering.

Wednesday 9

Today weather very wet and disagreeable which obliged us to remain in the hospital. At night my friend G. Lehman came from election furlough and of course we had a good time listening to the reports from the North with crying.

Thursday, November 10, 1864

Forenoon very busy as such a lot of men came in last night. This afternoon went to Chattanooga Depot and there saw some of 3rd Division 23rd Corps. Returns of election favorable for Abe and Andy Johnson.

Friday 11

Nothing of interest occurred, weather very pleasant. Several came from furlough today from different states.

Saturday, November 12, 1864

Forenoon kept very busy by reason of so many coming in from furlough. At night had a good chat with old friends til 10 o'clock.

Sunday 13

Busy cleaning up for inspection, afternoon went to Sunday school and had an excellent time. At night went to town where we heard a good sermon from (?) Apostles 8th Chapter. Weather very cool.

Monday, November 14, 1864

Forenoon busy in house, afternoon went to the city and thereabouts. Some of the 104th were at the Depot and went there and had a good visit with them and also learned that Capt. Bard was here. Saw lots of recruits going to the front. The pilgrims being ground out.

Tuesday 15

Had a very busy day, nothing of any interest. Tonight several came in from the front for which we had to get supper.

Wednesday, November 16, 1864

Today remained in hospital as it was very rainy. Today the Ohio boys returned from furlough. At night wrote a letter to Randolph. For the first time learned the destiny of Sherman's great raid. Received a paper from Nashville City.

Thursday 17

Weather very disagreeable on account of so much rain, a common occurrence in the South. Good news from Sherman today & great victory is expected from him. Nashville is all quiet.

Monday, November 18, 1864

Today a busy one and a very wet one, nothing of any interest except the good news from Sherman. All quiet tonight, busy reading & writing, received a letter and paper from home today.

Saturday 19

Busy cooking, we had an excellent dinner consisting of pudding and fish hash. Weather very rainy & disagreeable, tonight wrote a letter in answer to one. Received today good news from Sherman about the fall of Mobile. Remained in hospital.

Sunday, November 20, 1864

Forenoon busy with inspection, afternoon went in company with a friend to meeting and had a good time, although the march made it somewhat disagreeable. At night went to the Presbyterian Church and heard a good sermon.

Monday 21

Weather very cool with snow, did not get out of hospital. Good news from Sherman (?) expected tonight. Wrote a letter home and read from history. Tomorrow must prepare for Thanksgiving; it is so cold I can't write.

Tuesday, November 22, 1864

Today had nothing to do but did have a visitor. This afternoon began the slaughter of innocent turkeys & chickens for Thanksgiving dinner. For the first day this year the ground was frozen and tonight it is very cold.

Wednesday 23

Weather very cold, busy cleaning up and preparing for Thanksgiving dinner. Went to town this afternoon and tonight roasted turkeys. Great excitement over Sherman's victory and great results are expected from the General's victory.

Thursday, November 24, 1864

Today had great times and great preparations were made for a good dinner, which was served up at 12 Noon. This afternoon went to Chattanooga

Depot, tonight remained in the hospital reading & writing and expecting some music.

Friday 25

Today quiet, remained in hospital busy reading and at work. At night in company with some friends went to church and had an excellent meeting. Quite an alarm was produced by reason of (?).

Saturday, November 26, 1864

This morning our hospital library was opened and among the books were some of the best books ever published. All of the able-bodied men were enrolled today to prepare for emergencies produced by the threatened approach of Hood.

Sunday 27

Today busy reading & writing, at night was greatly disappointed by reason of an order prohibiting us from attending church. Wrote a letter home, everything full of excitement, we are now sitting around the table waiting.

Monday, November 28, 1864

Busy all day, remained in hospital all day reading from a good book entitled "Universal (?)". Weather very pleasant, several men came in from front wounded at Columbia.

Tuesday 29

Forenoon busy cooking, afternoon went to No. 14 Hospital to visit some of the Co. II boys but did not see them. Tonight a great excitement exists by reason of Hood's advance, news cheering.

Wednesday, November 30, 1864

Great excitement in hospital and in and around Nashville by reason of Hood's advance, a dreadful fight occurred at Franklin in which the 23rd Corp. was engaged. A great battle was fought near Franklin, Tennessee in which the 104th was engaged and resulted in the capture of 16 regimental flags from the Rebs. Two of them were captured by Co. II. They are to be presented & sent to Columbus, Ohio as trophies. The losses in Co. II were Capt.D.D. Bard, Corp. Williston, two Hallett boys.

Thursday, December 1

This morning our troops became alive in that a general fight is expected. Saw several of the 104th today and expect to visit them tomorrow. (?) (?) (?) is rejected today but it is not credited (???)

Friday, December 2, 1864

Busy this morning, at 9AM went to visit the 104th Regt. Had an excellent time but the boys were feeling very bad over the death of Capt. David Banks (?). Great excitement in Nashville over the advance of Hood's army.

Saturday 3

Forenoon busy at work, afternoon went to visit the front. Had a good time witnessing the advance of the Rebs on the place in force and saw the skir-

mishing which was quite (?) *at night. Fort Negley* …… (Illegible)

Sunday, December 4, 1864

Great excitement by reason of the gradual approach of the enemy, quite a long cannonading all day from our big guns. Tonight wrote a letter home and listened to the splendid music from our 23rd Corp. Band. Sunday spent in rather a busy way.

Monday 5

This morning went to Co. II and had a good visit, afternoon was paid off which was a welcome guest to us. Tonight in company with G.T. Lane reading & writing. Quite severe skirmishing occurred along our lines, today several being wounded and loss of life.

Tuesday, December 6, 1864

Heavy cannonading on the front. Had examination but did not have to go. Today busy in reading & writing, tonight wrote a letter, purchased an album and expect to have some more pictures.

Wednesday 7

This morning after performing the morning work went to visit the 122nd Regiment and had a good visit, about noon returned to work. Skirmishing was quite brisk today some fighting done by Negroes, tonight all was quiet and good opportunity for writing.

Thursday, December 8, 1864

Busy all day remained in hospital, weather very cold & disagreeable being outdoors. Nothing particular from the front except heavy skirmishing. Tonight all is quiet and all busy writing and reading, Hood yet in the vicinity.

Friday 9

Weather very cold remained in hospital all day. Afternoon drew some clothing preparatory to going home and made application for a furlough. Heavy skirmishing today, several contacts with Hood which we thought had gone into winter quarters.

Saturday, December 10, 1864

Today after doing my morning work went to visit the 4th Battery and had a good time. Weather very cold and disagreeable. News from the front indicates Hood's leaving the city which is credited in town tonight.

Sunday 11

Weather very cold staid in house all day, did not go to church. Nothing new from the front except Hood's leaving. Expected my furlough today but was disappointed. A force was sent out today to feel the enemy's position.

Monday, December 12, 1864

Weather very cold and disagreeable, remained in hospital all day. News from the front cheering, tonight our army has marching orders. Had visitor from the 122nd Ohio and had a good time. Battle expected tomorrow.

Tuesday 13

Weather moderated so this afternoon went out and saw a Division of Negroes fight Johnnies which resulted in finding the enemy in force. Tonight busy in reading & writing. Everyone looks forward to a speedy close of the war.

Wednesday, December 14, 1864

All quiet at the front, very little skirmishing. Paid a visit to Co. I and had a good visit with the boys. Orders were issued to the Corp. to be in readiness tomorrow morning. All quiet tonight, cooks busy preparing.

Thursday 15

Great excitement, today terrific cannonading all day & musketry at intervals but no results are yet learned. Remained in the hospital during the forenoon, afternoon went to town. Several wounded came in tonight. Many killed during the fray. Busy writing tonight.

Friday, December 16, 1864

The silence of the morn was broke by terrific cannonading; afternoon went out on an errand and saw the artillery fire. Admitted a large number in the hospital all disabled for lifetime, many died during the day, poor fellows.

Saturday 17

Aroused by the immense train of ambulances with our brave boys, quite a number came in today, most of them mortally wounded. Learned our army is still driving the enemy before them. Weather very rainy which makes it disagreeable for the art of marching. Tonight busy writing.

Sunday, December 18, 1864

Today very busy as we had such a large addition to our wounded numbers, did not go to church as every building is occupied for hospitals. News good from the front and a prospect of capturing most of Hood's army.

Monday 19

Very rainy almost impossible getting around for mud, had a busy day of it as we had such an addition to our numbers. Good news from the front which gives us encouragement that the cruel war will soon be over. Got a letter from home, folks all well.

Tuesday, December 20, 1864

Was busy all forenoon, afternoon went to town; everything presents a cheerful aspect by the sudden disappearance of the Johnnies. Never was manifested such a thankfulness to brave old General Thomas' men. Tonight busy reading & writing.

Wednesday 21

Today busy all day, remained in hospital taking care of wounded men, did last night until now. All *is quiet tonight except the busy scratching of the pen giving the details of the week. Snow today with ice.*

Thursday, December 22, 1864

Had nothing to do all day as the men were removed to No. 2 Hospital and preparations were made to receive Rebel wounded officers. Several came today including the number two Brig. General. Tonight my furlough was handed to me.

Friday 23

Started at 7AM on the train for Louisville, had a rough time as (?) *were reported on the tracks. Arrived at* (?) *8PM and crossed the river by Jeffersonville and found the train gone and reported to the Soldiers' Home.*

The pages for 12/24-31 are blank other than an illegible entry on 12/28.

Next comes section headed:

MEMORANDUM

(Some entries were continuations of notes from previous dates so I have moved them to the appropriate diary day)

Historical Facts

British Monarchy founded by William the Conqueror in 1066.

Annual income of Duke of Sutherland 360,000 pounds, Duke of Northumberland 300,000, Governor of Westminster 285,000.

On the next 4 pages he has written down quotes from Shakespeare, Burns etc. They are quite difficult to decipher so I have omitted.

On the following two pages there are pencil sketches of a women dressed in the Victorian garb of the time, including the bustle, feathered hat and parasol. **(See figure 15).**

The following 3 pages contain cash accounts of his expenditures. They are quite faded but I can tell you that washing cost $.05, "eatables" $.10 and stationary $.35.

The next page has more of the history of England starting with the accession of George V in 1820 through the revolt of the Bengal Army in 1858. I will skip the text as it is difficult to transcribe and not particularly relevant or interesting.

Next is *DEBTS TO JAMES ESSIG*

Martin Wolf	*$ .50*
H.L. Ensign	*1.00*
G. Benton	*.80*
L. Rodenbough	*.50*
D. Wise	*.80*
G.W. Hulette	*.20*
A.B. Hulette	*.10*
W. (?)	*.25*
A.G. Gamble	*.10*

On one of the Memorandum pages he started to list:

NAMES OF MEN COMPOSING 2ND SECTION
Enos Doughty
Robert Russell Sr.
Canavan (?) *Wayne*
Willie A. Lehman Indianapolis, Indiana

The End of the Diary Text

Figure 16 Camp Dennison near Cincinnati (ref. page 9 & 30)

Figure 17 Carver Hospital Washington (ref. page 36, 41 & 44)

Figure 18 Soldiers Rest Washington D.C. (ref. page 42)

Figure 19 Lincoln Hospital Washington (ref. page 51)

Figure 20 Hospital #2 Nashville (ref. page 64)

Figure 21 Presbyterian Church later Hospital #8 Nashville (ref. page 66)

Figure 22 State House Nashville (ref. page 72)

Figure 23 Nashville – Chattanooga Depot with State House in background (ref. page 79)

His Life after the War

Education

Great Grandfather Essig was discharged from the Army June 17, 1865 and returned to Ohio. He enrolled in Mount Union College in Alliance, Ohio and graduated with the class of 1869 receiving a degree of "Bachelor of Science for the Science Curriculum", according to Joanne Houmard a researcher at the Mt. Union College Library with whom I exchanged emails. She further reported that their records show that in 1872 James enrolled in the Commercial and Actual Business Department of Mount Union and received an SM or Master of Science degree in 1872. The records show him living in Randolph, Elmore and Carrollton, Ohio.

Another document from 1872 says: "He has been at Mount Union, Stark Co. for four years since his discharge, two years in Sandusky County, Ohio, and one year in Columbiana County, Ohio". It went on to say "and the remainder of the time in Stark Co., Ohio" but this was crossed out. It further added that he was a student and teacher during this period.

Almost all of the later documents show him residing in Carrollton in Carroll County, Ohio.

After college he became a full-time teacher at Union Schools where he eventually became Superintendent of the Union School System. Mt. Union College records list him as a teacher and merchant. I find no other reference to him being a merchant. **See figure 24 photo.**

Family

On August 13, 1869 James was married to Elizabeth F. McCormick by the Reverend John Wright, M.E. (Methodist) Minister, in Hanoverton, Columbiana County, Ohio. This information was obtained from a copy of the marriage record and from written statements from Essig. **See figure 25 marriage certificate.**

A document **(see figure 1)** signed by James in 1915 shows the following children, living or dead:

Emma See Essig born May 20, 1870
Mary Anderson Essig born March 5, 1872
Anna Grace Essig born August 23, 1875
Lillian Alice Essig born August 3, 1882

And last but certainly not least was my grandmother:

Laura Gaily Essig born November 2, 1886 **(see figure 27)**

Sadly, another document signed by James in 1898 lists only two children still living, Emma See Horn (or Howe?) nee Essig and Laura whom he shows born in 1887, not 1886 as he stated in the 1915 document.

Essig's Health

James suffered greatly the rest of his life from his wound which caused his health to steadily deteriorate. The National Archive military and pension records contain dozens of documents relating to his disability including applications, medical exams, testimonials, personal statements, etc. It appears his first military invalid pension was awarded at a rate of $4 per month from June 18, 1865 ending May 11, 1872.

The records show that in his early years he stood 5'11" and weighed around 190. One physician notes that he comes from a large strong muscular family. He steadily deteriorated due to complications from his wound which is documented in later examinations. In an 1892 disability exam his height was shown as 5'10" and his weight as 122 at age 51. His pension at this time was $16 a month. During that exam he stated:

"I have constant pain all over my face and head, about 4-5 days of the week the pain is intense so that I am unfit to attend to anything. The head is so sensitive that I am unable to rest at night. The softest pillow seems hard. I am totally disabled from performing any manual labor."

Doctors' statements stated his disability to be on a par with the loss of an arm or leg. One of his attending physicians related that he was at one time a pupil in classes taught by Mr. Essig and that there were times when teacher Essig would have to leave the room due to his headaches or when his wound was draining. Apparently the future doctor was often put in charge of the class during these occurrences.

He must have regained his health to some degree in his later years as we have photos of him, including one of him holding my mother around 1913 **(see figures 26 & 28)** and he is not the emaciated person described in the 1892 document.

In 1890 his pension was increased to $16 **(see figure 29)**. Effective June 29, 1892 his pension was again increased this time to $30 per month until his death May 3, 1918 at the age of 77. According to the death certificate **(see figure 30)** he passed away at City Hospital in Alliance, OH, having been admitted on April 29, 1918. The cause of death is listed as "Apoplexy", which is a Greek word for seizure, so it is likely he died from a stroke or cerebral hemorrhage. The secondary cause was shown as arterial sclerosis.

All of the many affidavits and testimonials contained in the records testify that Essig had no vices and was a most honorable and upstanding person. At one time I had a formal document signed by General Irving MacDowell (Lincoln's first Commanding General who was replaced after the loss at Bull Run) appointing Essig to, as I recall, an honorary Colonel in the Grand Army of the Republic or The Army of the Potomac, and dated, I think, in the 1870s. This leads me to speculate that he was active in one or more veteran organizations. To date my search has not located the document which was rolled up in a cardboard tube.

In addition, mother often spoke of seeing his uniform and sword in the attic at one of her childhood homes. This may have been a ceremonial outfit which has been lost. I do have his gold-topped ebony walking stick with his signature "*J. B. Essig*" engraved on the top. I also have in my possession his wife's Elgin gold pendant watch engraved "**E.M. Essig**". The watch is in perfect running condition and, as far as I know, has never been cleaned or repaired.

Carrollton & Dubuque

His last residence appears to have been North Lisbon St. in Carrollton, Ohio.

Records indicate that Elizabeth Essig moved very soon after his death to 37 Nevada St. in Dubuque, Iowa. However, there is a bit of a mystery surrounding the move to Dubuque. I have letters and postcards showing that James' daughter Laura having married Austin Louis Wertz was residing at 1564 Iowa St. in Dubuque in November, 1913 when my mother, Elizabeth Gertrude Wertz was born. There is a letter postmarked in Canton, OH from Austin's mother, Mrs. Frantz (2nd marriage name), offering congratulations on the birth and sending their love to Mr. & Mrs. Essig, implying that they were also in Dubuque.

There are later cards addressed to the Wertz family in 1919 at the same 37 Nevada St. address in Dubuque as well as one in 1916 to 235 Nevada St. Yet, I also have one addressed to my mother in Carrollton, OH postmarked in Dubuque May 29, 1917.

To make matters even more confusing, I have a card from Austin Wertz addressed to his wife at 1132 Spring Ave. Canton, OH dated 11/3/20. However, I also have a letter from Laura Wertz to her daughters Betty (Elizabeth) and Laura in 1922 which implies that they were living in Dubuque. In the letter both Austin & Laura were on their way back to Dubuque and noted that their daughters were being well-cared for, during their absence, by nuns at a convent. Go figure, I guess more research is needed to unravel the Dubuque connection and timeline.

-END-

Figure 24 Undated photo of J.B. Essig (ref. page 104)

Copy of Marriage Record

THE STATE OF OHIO, } ss. PROBATE COURT
COLUMBIANA COUNTY

I, S. W. CRAWFORD, *Judge of said Probate Court, hereby certify that the following is a correct copy of the Marriage Record of said Court as to the Marriage of the persons named in said copy:*

RETURN.

The State of Ohio, } ss
Columbiana County,

I certify, that on the 13th day of August, A. D., 1869 Mr. James B. Essig and Miss Elizabeth F. McCormick were, by me, legally joined in Marriage.

John Wright, Minister.

Rec'd. and recorded Sept. 10th, 1869.

S. J. Firestone, P. J.

Witness *my signature and the seal of said Court, at Lisbon, Ohio, this* 21" *day of* May, *A. D. 19*18.

S.W. Crawford
Probate Judge and Ex-Officio Clerk of Said Court

Figure 25 Marriage Certificate (ref. page 105)

Figure 26 Undated Photo of James Essig (ref. page 106)

Figure 27 James' wife Elizabeth McCormick Essig with daughter Laura (Amba) – ref. page 105)

Figure 28 J.B. Essig with granddaughter Elizabeth (Mom) – ref. page 106)

№ 123,308 Increase.

UNITED STATES OF AMERICA

DEPARTMENT OF THE INTERIOR

BUREAU OF PENSIONS

It is hereby certified That in conformity with the laws of the United States James Essig who was a Corporal Co. I. 104" Regiment Ohio Volunteer Infantry. is entitled to a pension at the rate of Sixteen dollars per month, to commence on the eighth day of January one thousand eight hundred and ninety This Pension being for "Gunshot wound of left cheek."

Given at the Department of the Interior this seventeenth day of March one thousand eight hundred and ninety and of the Independence of the United States of America the one hundred and fourteenth

John W. Noble
Secretary of the Interior.

Countersigned:
Green B Raum
Commissioner of Pensions.

Former payments covering any portion of the same time to be deducted.

Figure 29 Pension doc. 1890 (ref. page 106)

STATE OF OHIO
SECRETARY OF STATE
BUREAU OF VITAL STATISTICS
COLUMBUS, OHIO

No. 3102

I, J. E. MONGER, State Registrar of Vital Statistics, do hereby certify the following to be a true and correct copy of the Certificate of Death for J. B. Essig on file in The Central Bureau of Vital Statistics of Ohio.

PLACE OF DEATH
County of Stark
Township of .... Registration District No. 1208 File No. 34518
or
Village of .... Primary Registration District No. 8481 Registered No. 138
or
City of Alliance (No. City Hospital St., 4th Ward) [If death occurred in a hospital or institution, give its NAME instead of street and number.]

2 FULL NAME J. B. Essig

PERSONAL AND STATISTICAL PARTICULARS

3 SEX Male
4 COLOR OR RACE White
5 SINGLE, MARRIED, WIDOWED OR DIVORCED (Write the word) Married
6 DATE OF BIRTH Sept. (Month) 18 (Day), 1841 (Year)
7 AGE 77 yrs. 7 mos. 15 ds. If LESS than 1 day, ...hrs. or ......min.?
8 OCCUPATION (a) Trade, profession, or particular kind of work Retired
(b) General nature of industry, business, or establishment in which employed (or employer) Farmer
9 BIRTHPLACE (State or country) Ohio
PARENTS
10 NAME OF FATHER William Essig
11 BIRTHPLACE OF FATHER (State or country) Penna.
12 MAIDEN NAME OF MOTHER Rebecca Rimus
13 BIRTHPLACE OF MOTHER (State or country) Not known
14 THE ABOVE IS TRUE TO THE BEST OF MY KNOWLEDGE
(Informant) Mrs. J. B. Essig
(Address) Carrolton, Ohio
15 Filed May 9, 1918 J. F. Hogan Registrar

MEDICAL CERTIFICATE OF DEATH

16 DATE OF DEATH May (Month) 3 (Day), 1918 (Year)
17 I HEREBY CERTIFY, That I attended deceased from 4/29, 1918, to May 3, 1918, that I last saw him alive on May 3, 1918, and that death occurred, on the date stated above, at 6 P.m.
The CAUSE OF DEATH* was as follows:
Apoplexy
(Duration) ......yrs. ......mos. 1 ds.
Contributory (Secondary) Arterial Sclerosis
(Duration) ......yrs. ......mos. ......ds.
(Signed) H. C. Manchester, M. D.
May 4, 1918 (Address) Alliance, O.
*State the Disease Causing Death, or, in deaths from Violent Causes, state (1) Means of Injury; and (2) whether Accidental, Suicidal, or Homicidal.
18 LENGTH OF RESIDENCE (For Hospitals, Institutions, Transients, or Recent Residents)
At place of death ......yrs. ......mos. 2 ds. In the State ......yrs. ......mos. ......ds.
Where was disease contracted, If not at place of death? Carrolton, O.
Former or usual residence Carrolton, O.
19 PLACE OF BURIAL OR REMOVAL Carrolton, Ohio
DATE OF BURIAL May 7, 1918
20 UNDERTAKER J. A. Shaw & Son Co.
ADDRESS Alliance, O.

IN TESTIMONY WHEREOF, I have hereunto subscribed my name and caused my official seal to be affixed, at Columbus, this 29th day of June, in the year of our Lord one thousand nine hundred and 18

J. E. Monger
State Registrar.

PENSION OFFICE JUL 12 1918 U. S.

Figure 30 Certificate of Death (ref. page 107)

ACKNOWLEDGEMENTS
&
PERMISSIONS

I owe a great debt to my much-loved late mother for being the "historian" in the family and holding on to so many of these records and passing them down to us. In addition, I owe thanks to my late beloved aunt and mother's sister, Virginia Hurd, who helped fill in many blanks during my last visit with her.

A special thanks to my wonderful wife, Peggy, for encouraging me to undertake this project and for her sincere interest, patient advice and assistance. Also my daughter, Rachel "The Reader", provided much appreciated last minute proofreading.

The Internet was invaluable in tracking down so much of this information and many of the photos and illustrations. There's so much more out there to be discovered, it takes a lot of time and patience. The National Archives are, of course, an amazing wealth of information even if you do have to fill out a number of forms and applications to obtain them through the mail. One day, perhaps, you will be able to access the records online.

I need to acknowledge the various staff members at the Nashville Public Library and The Nashville Historical Society for answering many of my questions when I visited in the the autumn of 2006.

Many thanks also go to Joanne Houmard, from the Mount Union College Library in Ohio. She was an excellent source of information on Essig's life after the War.

I wish to thank Paul W. Gilbert owner of "Michigan Views" for his excellent work in restoring the original Civil War tintype of my great grandfather. He specializes in historic photographs and performs excellent work at reasonable prices.

A wonderful resource is the "Guide to Civil War Nashville" published by the Battle of Nashville Preservation Society and written by Mark Zimmerman. Many of the pictures included here came from one or more of their web sites. They are figure numbers 12, 20, 21, 22 and 23 for which kind permission was granted by James D. Kay, Jr.

Figure 7 Minie Balls was credited to Jerry Morris and taken from the web site "Weapons and Ammunition of the Confederate Soldier". However I was unable to locate Jerry Morris to request permission.

Figures 9 and 11 are Kurz & Allison paintings dating to 1891, from the internet. I was unable to find anyone with the rights to seek permission. Figures 10 and 17 came from www.civilwar.net web site which contains an amazing treasure trove of Civil War photos. It is the site's belief that these images are part of the public domain due to their age and that they are located in the Library of Congress.

Figure 16 "Camp Dennison-Taken from Old Aunt Roady's Hill" was "Drawn by Johnson in the Zoauve Lt. Guard, Company A" and permission was granted by Jace Delgado of JRD Photography.

Figure 18 Soldiers Rest, Washington D.C. is from an 1864 lithograph by Charles Magnus. I was unable to find any person to request permission so I assume this is also now part of the public domain. Figures 8 &19 were copied from the internet and no rights or source were discovered. Included with figure 8 "Rebel Charge on Ft. Sanders" is from the Archives of Michigan.

I encourage others, especially family members to build on this short biography as there is a lot more to be learned.

Lastly, it is with eternal gratitude that I thank my Great Grandfather James B. Essig for his sacrifice for his country and for writing the Diary. In many ways so much would not have been possible without him.

Thomas A. Marquard
Dearborn, Michigan
July, 2008

INDEX

www.ingramcontent.com/pod-product-compliance
Ingram Content Group UK Ltd.
Pitfield, Milton Keynes, MK11 3LW, UK
UKHW041939190726
13854UKWH00004B/1682